To Tammy:
dedication to
very proud l...

John F. Davidson
1-7-07

The Toy Fox
TERRIER
···Wired ··for ··Action ···

John F. Davidson

A revision of The Toy Fox Terrier
by Eliza L. Hopkins and Cathy J. Flamholtz

Alpine
PUBLICATIONS
Loveland, Colorado

The Toy Fox Terrier: Wired for Action

Copyright 2006 by John F. Davidson
Parts of this publication were originally published as *The Toy Fox Terrier* by Eliza L. Hopkins and Cathy J. Famholtz, copyright 1988 by OTR Publications. Revised with permission.

All rights reserved. No part of this book may be used or reproduced in any manner whatsoever, including electronic media or photocopying, without written permission from the publisher, except in the case of brief quotations embodied in critical reviews. For permission, write to Alpine Publications, Inc., P.O. Box 7027, Loveland, CO 80537.

Library of Congress Cataloging-in-Publication Data

Davidson, John L., 1946-
  The toy fox terrier, wired for action / John L. Davidson.
     p. cm.
  ISBN 1-57779-077-4
1. Toy fox terrier. I. Title.

  SF429.T73D38 2006
  636.76--dc22   2005054837

Many manufacturers secure trademark rights for their products. When Alpine Publications is aware of a trademark claim, we print the product name as trademarked or in initial capital letters.

Alpine Publications accepts no responsibility for any errors, inaccuracies or omissions. The reader is advised to check with their local, licensed veterinarian regarding any medical advice. Any slights of people or organizations are unintentional.

Cover Photo: Ch. Jacobs Mystique of Doogit, owned by Dorothy Fisher and bred by Dot Jacobs. Photo © Digi-Art, Pocomoke, MD, and Gr. Ch. 'PR' Meadowood's Got Notion owned and bred by Dr. John Davidson.
Back Cover Photo: Simone, Jeannine, Viper and Thais owned by David Ring and Jud Guillot. Photo © sandephoto.com.
Title Page Photo: Gr. Ch. 'PR' Meadowood's Got a Notion, owned by John F. Davidson.

Design and layout: Laura Newport

1 2 3 4 5 6 7 8 9 0

Printed in the United States of America.

DEDICATION

This book is the culmination of my 35 years of experience with Toy Fox Terriers. I did not achieve this longevity and modest success alone. The encouragement and counsel of my wife, Sally, has enabled me to enjoy breeding and showing TFTs after all these years. I continue to extensively draw upon her knowledge and experience as a nurse. Her patience, sense of humor, and rationality have enriched our partnership. Most importantly, whether in the ring or out, she has made it fun to be involved in the sport of dogs. With great affection, I dedicate this book to Sally Davidson.

John F. Davidson
September 25, 2005

THE TOY FOX TERRIER

By Anne Gendron

There is no other creature to give one's heart a stir
As the fun-lov'n natured, Toy Fox Terrier
He is a canine gentleman yet sassy as can be
No stranger is known, always at home
His purpose is to please

You may find him playing, running or chasing butterflies
Or romping with his shadow as the sun falls from the sky
No fear is found in him, he's as brave as brave could be
Six pounds of courage gently wrapped
And tied with loyalty

If your life should lack for something
And you need some kind of friend
To bring you joy and happiness
To stand by you to the end
Please do not worry, for your answer is so clear
Open your heart to this gift of love
—The Toy Fox Terrier

Owned by Anne Gendron.

TABLE OF CONTENTS

INTRODUCTION

The Toy Fox Terrier was written by Eliza L. Hopkins and Cathy J. Flamholtz and published in 1988 by OTR Publications. Mrs. Hopkins has been an outstanding breeder of Toy Fox Terriers for 45 years and is an accepted authority on the breed. Mrs. Flamholtz is an excellent writer with several canine books to her credit. Mrs. Flamholtz wrote, "While the words in the book are mine, they are born out of Eliza's extensive experience." It was a brilliant collaboration. Their book was and remains the only true breed book available on the Toy Fox Terrier.

Much has happened in the world of TFTs since 1988. The book had gone through three printings and the publisher was no longer active. The supply of available books had dwindled to fewer than twenty when I inquired of both authors whether a revised edition would be forthcoming. Neither of them was eager for another project right now, but expressed confidence that I might do the job.

I purchased the rights to the book in 2004 and set about updating and revising the work. Only two chapters remain intact: *TFT Character* and *The TFT in Obedience*. The chapters on *TFT History* and *Understanding the Standard* have been updated to reflect the breed's acceptance into the American Kennel Club. Seven chapters dealing with breeding the TFT and raising puppies have been revised to reflect my experience as a 35-year breeder of TFTs and as an AKC and UKC judge of the breed. *The Versatile TFT* chapter now has additional profiles of TFTs in agility, flyball, therapy, and seizure alert work. The first research on the genetics of the breed is offered in the appendix. These articles by Dr. Ralph Rascati, a university teacher and researcher in genetics for 25 years, are a valuable first step in understanding the genetics of the breed.

Though revised, I have sought to maintain the style of the original work. Reading that book was like having a conversation with a mentor, an unpretentious and valuable sharing of every aspect of the breed. Perhaps more so for me, since Eliza has mentored me now for 35 years! The result is our collective 80 years of experience in the breed.

THE TOY FOX TERRIER
WIRED FOR ACTION!

The feisty nature of these diminutive dogs gives them not only a longevity few dogs can claim, but also the guts to tackle tasks seemingly beyond their abilities.

These little dogs relish most any challenge put before them. Judy Guillot, a wheelchair user in Tucson, Arizona, has such a dog. Her Toy Fox Terrier helps her get ready for work by fetching her shoes and picking up whatever she drops. Even though her dog was the smallest dog to be certified, Guillot's terrier finished first in her class of Handi-Dogs.

A state trooper in Illinois who worries about his wife's safety when he works nights has trained his Toy Fox Terrier to bark whenever a stranger sets foot on his property. With his police science background, he knows that the noise a small dog creates can be as menacing to an intruder as the bark or presence of a larger breed.

A major circus production features a Toy Fox Terrier, amidst a group of Poodles, performing difficult feats such as walking a high wire and jumping from a basket 20 feet in the air into his trainer's arms. Later, a clown roams the crowd while a small black and white terrier peers out of his pocket at the spectators.

In rural Kansas a farmer decides that his wife's "housebaby," a TFT, should earn his keep and takes the little terrier to his rat infested silo. At first cowering, old instincts are awakened as the terrier grabs a rat by the neck and shakes it.

In the hills of Tennessee, a pack of TFTs, what hill country folks refer to as *feists*, prove indefatigable in treeing squirrels and jumping rabbits.

In a Tennessee nursing home, a frail hand reaches out to pet Booger, a certified therapy dog. He is her only visitor each week.

It is the Toy Fox Terrier's temperament and intelligence that attract loyalists. The TFT's intelligence is legendary. This traditional circus dog learns quickly and is eager to please. The Toy Fox Terrier looks into your eyes as if trying to read your mind and tries as hard as he can to talk to you. Veteran owners often find themselves spelling words to keep their TFT off guard. If you're looking for a little trembling toy to protect, the TFT is not for you. Although they will settle down as they mature, as puppies they are dynamos. I once described a puppy to his new owner as a firecracker; this owner later said a torpedo would have been a more accurate description.

No shrinking violet, this toy breed is above all a terrier:

Alert,

   Sassy . . .

      and wired for action!

TFT HISTORY

The Toy Fox Terrier of today is an all-American breed. His roots, however, lie across the sea in merry old England. It has been a long genesis from the unkempt, scruffy dogs that were first labeled terriers to the handsome, sleek toy dogs seen in today's show rings. In the beginning, terriers were the working companions of British farmers. They aided rural homesteaders in ridding their lands of unwanted vermin. Later, when the small dogs became an integral part of the sport of foxhunting, the Smooth Fox Terrier was born. When styles in foxhunting changed, the little terrier seemed doomed. He was saved by the era of dog shows and kennels clubs. Within a few short years, he had soared to the top of British show circles. Americans grew to appreciate the Smooth Fox Terrier, too. He became a fixture in American show rings and one of the most popular breeds in the country. The TFT has been called the "little brother of the Smooth Fox Terrier." That he is, and he still retains the qualities that propelled the Fox Terrier to prominence.

EARLY TERRIERS (1500's - 1700's)

We do not know how long terriers have existed in Great Britain. We do know that they date back as far as Julius Caesar's day. Scribes reported that there were "small dogs that would follow their quarry to ground." The 15th century book, *Field Sports,* contained a mention of these dogs. The terrier was described by Dr. Caius, personal physician to Queen Elizabeth I, in the first dog book, written in 1557. Dr. Caius was primarily responsible for the appellation "terrier," which comes from the Latin *terra,* meaning "earth."

By the 1600's, England's kings were hunting with terriers. In a letter dated August 15, 1617, King James I asked a friend to secure terriers for the royal kennels. He requested the Laird of Caldwell "to search out and send to us two couples of excellent terriers or earth dogs, which are both stout fox killers and will stay in the ground."

1

In speaking of those early terriers, one of the American's first Fox Terrier breeders, August Belmont, said, "The characteristics of the Terrier...were...a natural inclination to hunt and destroy vermin of any kind, pursuing it to its refuge wherever it be within the Terrier's power to reach it; this trait being accompanied by a sprightly and tense nature, keen sense of hearing, quick vision, a most unerring nose, and an indomitable gameness."

"Being intended to hunt with his master, he should be ready and eager to attack the object of the hunt, enter into its hiding place and indicating the locality by giving tongue or drawing out the game in the open...This style of hunting and fighting requires great dash, courage and dexterity."

FOXHUNTING AND THE BIRTH OF THE FOX TERRIER (late 1700's - mid 1800's)

Originally, fox hunting was necessary, since this cunning critter was a formidable predator of small livestock. By the 1800's, foxhunting came to be regarded as a gentleman's sport. Sportsmen had discovered that chasing the fleet fox through woods and across meadows, provided an ideal day's entertainment. Foxhounds, excelling in tracking ability and endowed with melodious voices, were developed specifically for use in the hunt. The sly fox was not to be outdone. To avoid capture, he would dart into a hole. Here he would snuggle safe and secure, while the frustrated hunters and their hounds milled above ground. Such resourcefulness put a prompt end to the day's sport.

Enter the terrier. It was discovered that the vermin dogs, so common on British farms, fit easily into foxholes. With their keen noses and abundant courage, they could cause the fox to bolt. The hounds and hunters could then, once again, take up the chase. Certainly, many a terrier saved the day's sport for the hunters. It was important that the terrier refrain from killing the fox, for this would have put a quick end to the day's outing. His purpose was to cause the fox to flee, or barring that, to pinpoint its location underground by barking. The hunters could then come to the dog's aid, and dig the terrier and his quarry from the hole. The little dogs became an important adjunct to the sport. "No foxhound establishment was considered complete without a brace of well-bred terriers," wrote Bewick in his 1790 book, *History of Quadrapeds.*

Foxhound kennels often employed a "terrier man," whose sole purpose was to attend to the terriers. He made sure that the dogs were on the spot when needed. In smaller establishments, the head groom sometimes served this purpose. While long legged terriers, capable of keeping up with the hounds, were sometimes employed, small terriers were often used. They were carried in leather bags, suspended from the saddle or slung across the terrier man's shoulder. Because of this practice, small terriers were often dubbed "the groom's pocket piece."

These early Fox Terriers varied greatly in type. The foxhunters cared not what the dog looked like, so long as he could perform afield. But, like all sportsmen, foxhunters were a competitive lot. Many an evening was spent recapping past hunting adventures, and word of a particularly adept dog spread quickly. A premium was paid for the puppies of a proficient hunter and he would be in demand as a stud. Selective breeding, based on performance, was widely practiced. Writing in the 1800's, John Walker described his visit to a Fox Terrier kennel. The proprietor, then eighty years of age, had been developing his strain of Fox Terriers for the past forty years. "Pedigree and blood have been held subservient to unflinching courage; for wherever the slightest indisposition was manifested to go at anything when told to do so, that specific animal was not permitted to perpetuate his or her species, and its canine form did not long annoy the eye of the owner nor disgrace his kennel."

To the best of our knowledge, the first Fox Terriers carried the blood of England's old Black and Tan Terrier. As the competitive fever to breed the best terriers escalated, hunters tried a variety of crossbreedings. Greyhound, Beagle and Bull Terrier blood was introduced. The Bull Terrier cross was, by far, the most controversial. Most owners decried this cross, for they felt that it gave the dog too much fight and caused him to engage the fox in combat, rather than flushing it.

Early Fox Terriers came in a wide variety of colors. In 1790, Bewick describes the myriad of colors available to the hunter. "Terriers of the best blood...are now, by the prevalence of fashion, bred of all colours, red, black (with tanned faces, flanks, feet and legs) and brindle-sandy; some few brown-pied, white-pied, and pure white." A new age was dawning, however. Fashion dictated that a good Fox Terrier was to be prominently white in color. We are told that this attribute had a practical purpose. It was said that the hounds, on occasion, mistook the terrier for the fox and promptly tore it asunder. Bewick suggests, however, that it was the young sportsmen who had trouble discerning the difference between the fox and the dog. Nevertheless, white color quickly won favor and became the hallmark of a good Fox Terrier.

Nat. Gr. CH. "PR" Rinebold's Winkie,
owned by Rinebold Kennels.

The appropriate size for a Fox Terrier has always been a hotly debated topic. In general, most Fox Terriers fell within the 10 - 20 pounds range, as a dog larger than this was considered too big to go to ground effectively. We do know that smaller Fox Terriers coexisted with their larger brethren. In 1867, the prominent writer Stonehenge reported, the "dog may weigh from 6 pounds to 10 pounds, or even 20 pounds; but provided he is large enough for his calling, he cannot be too small. It is an advantage to keep down the size of certain dogs as much as possible, and to consider that two small terriers will do more than double the work of one large dog, whilst they consume no more..."

After the 1830's, the sport of foxhunting changed radically. Many of Britain's forests were cleared and, with more open land, foxhunting became a faster sport. The fox was easier to locate on the deforested land. More men signed on with hunt clubs and mounted their horses for the thrilling chase. Capturing a fox became a secondary consideration, for the real fun was riding at breakneck speed across the newly formed meadows. If a fox went to ground, the hunters might inquire if there was a terrier at the nearest farmstead. If a dog could not be found, it was back on the horses and off again. "Modern hunting, quick gallops and the go-aheadedness of the times have done away with the Fox Terrier's occupation," lamented the dog writer, Rawdon Lee. By 1840, Blaine commented sadly, "The occupation of the Fox Terrier is almost gone."

While no longer fundamental to foxhunting, the Fox Terrier was still admired on British farms. As in days of old, he maintained a position of prominence as a vermin dog *par excellence*. Idstone, author of the early work *The Dog*, was an outspoken advocate of the Fox Terrier's work in this capacity. "Every fox-terrier ought to be a good vermin killer," he said in an 1860 letter to the British publication, *The Field*. "Only about one man in five hundred wants a terrier to run with hounds; but he wants a vermin dog, and if the dog does run with hounds, he must be a 'rat-trap' all the same. I admire beauty much, but I have a far greater respect for character and quality, and I prefer a rough diamond to a polished pebble."

THE RAPID RISE OF THE SMOOTH FOX TERRIER (1860's - early 1900's)

With the decline in foxhunting, the Fox Terrier's future was in peril. It's true the breed could still be seen on farms, but the serious selective breeding had long been dominated by foxhunters. Fortunately for the breed, the dog show movement was dawning. Propelled along with this heady new avocation was the little foxhunting terrier. The rise of the Smooth Fox Terrier had officially begun. During those early days, there was no official standard. Therefore, the dogs which graced British show rings were of widely varying types. Indeed, almost any dog of primarily white color, with black and tan markings and a docked tail, was entered as a Fox Terrier. Very quickly, however, the establishments which had long bred terriers to accompany foxhound packs, established themselves as the ones to beat in the show ring. The kennels of Oakely, Quorn, Belvoir and Grove set the standards for excellence in the breed.

The first separate classes for Smooth Fox Terriers were offered in 1863. The breed took the fledgling show world by storm. There was a dramatic rise in support. In 1864, forty Fox Terriers appeared at the Nottingham show. By 1867 and 1868, the entries rose to 62. Several years later at Nottingham, the Smooth Fox Terrier entry was an astounding 270!

It's unlikely that the dog world of that time had seen anything like the boom of the Smooth Fox Terrier. He was immediately embraced by dog show fanciers. Soon he was a popular subject of prominent artists. While little attention had previously been paid to his pedigree, it was now proudly recorded in the newly established stud books of England's Kennel Club. An incredible demand sprang up for Smooth Fox Terrier puppies and breeding stock, and fantastic sums were paid for winning dogs. A club was formed to foster the breed and a magazine devoted exclusively to the Fox Terrier was established.

THE TOY TERRIERS

By the late 1800's, the dog show era was firmly underway. Another movement was afoot in England, too. The late 1800's became "the heyday of Toy Dogdom." Fashionable women, and an occasional gentleman, took pride in being seen with a toy dog in their arms. As we've seen, small Smooth Fox Terriers had existed in England. Even in the very earliest dog shows, small Fox Terriers made a showing. One writer of the time, in discussing the diversity of size in Smooth Fox Terriers, tells us that some shows had "classes of small dogs deserving rather to be placed in a class for toys."

Stonehenge, in the 1887 edition of *The Dog in Health and Disease*, devotes a section to toy terriers. He describes the "black-tan, smooth," now known as the Toy Manchester, and the Yorkshire Terrier. Interestingly, he also mentions a toy verison of the "fox terrier, which last are now frequently made such by young ladies of the present day. All these breeds, when toys, have the same points as their larger brethren, and differ only in weight, which should not exceed 5 or 6 pounds, at most."

So, we find that a Toy Fox Terrier actually existed in Great Britain in the 1800's. Why this toy version did not survive will forever remain a mystery. Certainly, one would have thought that, with the booming popularity of the Smooth Fox Terrier, this diminutive brother would have been an instant success. Instead, the ultimate creation of a Toy Fox Terrier would be left to enterprising American fancies.

THE FOX TERRIER IN AMERICA

The first Fox Terriers arrived in this country in the late 1800's or early 1900's. They were an immediate success. Show fanciers discovered that the natty Smooth Fox Terrier was a formidable competitor in show rings. Farmers joined the British homesteader in admiring their vermin catching qualities. Youngsters begged their parents for a Smooth Fox Terrier, and the breed became an esteemed child's companion. The breed became so popular that the RCA Victor Company chose the Smooth to grace its logo, "His Master's Voice."

Runts from Smooth Fox Terrier litters became popular. They gained a reputation as the scrappiest and boldest of the lot. They were often called "Fyce" or "Fiest" dogs, testament to their feisty natures. Though small in size, owners found a multitude of uses for these mighty mites. They performed the traditional ratting functions, and joined the farmer in hunting squirrels and rabbits. Sometimes, they were even allowed to accompany the larger Coonhounds on night hunts.

The late Howard Currens, one of our prominent TFT breeders, remembered these dogs from his childhood. With great fondness he recalled a rat hunt, staged one Sunday. "The handlers would poke the rats from under the old log houses and the little dogs would catch them. When the day ended the dogs had accounted for 74 rodents."

This important photo from the 1920's gives clues to the TFT's origin. These small Fox Terriers, who matured at 10-12 pounds, were owned by Lester Schuyler, father of current TFT fancier, Sky Hughes. The puppies are shown with fresh deer antlers. It was from small Fox Terriers, such as these, that TFT was developed.

Frank Davidson and his hunting terrier, Clown. Circa 1930.

Valued for their superior intelligence these diminutive Fox Terriers sometimes served as canine entertainers. In the early days of this century, there was little entertainment for rural dwellers. Small circuses, sometimes called Dog and Pony shows, toured regionally. Very often, the dog chosen was the little Fox Terrier. He amazed audiences with his antics and gained a reputation for charm, agility and verve.

THE HARD ROAD TO RECOGNITION

The United Kennel Club began registering the Smooth Fox Terrier in 1912. Early Toy Fox Terriers, despite their small size, were registered with the UKC as Smooth Fox Terriers. However, in the mid-1920's, fanciers approached the UKC seeking a separate and distinct category for their toy dogs. It took many years before they achieved their objective. Writing in 1961, Dr. E. G. Fuhrman, an early supporter of the TFT, recalled, "The breed did not come about overnight as many seem to think, but through the efforts of many years, hard ones..." On February 24, 1936, official recognition was granted under the name Toy Fox Terrier. The first litter, composed of a single pup, was registered on February 24, 1936, by Mrs. I. H. Young, of Punxsutawney, Pennsylvania. On February 28, 1936, Mrs. E. T. Rosengrant, of Crichton, Alabama, registered a litter of two. "Finally the Toy was definitely established," Dr. Fuhrman recalls. "The hardest part was over with and now there was enough breeding stock to assure a continuation of the Toy Fox Terrier."

Today, the Toy Fox Terrier breeds so true to type that it's difficult for us to imagine the difficulties and hardships faced by those early breed pioneers. In those formative years, size was a grave concern in TFT circles. An article in a 1959 issue of *Bloodlines* said, "One of the constant battles is to keep the Toy Fox Terrier a true Toy breed of dog. We have those that want a larger type... any great variation in weight and size can be accomplished in a short period of time towards the Standard Size Fox Terrier... to go to the small size takes years..."

A photo from the 1950's. This five pound male is Riley's Little Jody, owned by Mr. and Mrs. Arvin Riley, of Crooksville, Ohio.

Those dedicated to the true Toy Fox Terrier, however, valiantly fought all attempts to make the TFT into a larger breed. Fortunately, they had the wholehearted support of the United Kennel Club. Dr. Fuhrman said, "Along the way there were a few who tried by nearly every means... to change the breed, to destroy it... and breed for bigger dogs than the Toy Standard called for. The real breeders fought this movement tooth and nail along with *Bloodlines Journal* and the United Kennel Club won each battle for the survival of the Toy Fox Terrier breed."

Another problem plagued those early breeders. It had been firmly established that the Toy Fox Terrier would indeed remain a toy. This took concerted efforts on the part of breeders, for they had to eliminate oversize dogs from their breeding programs. Some breeders, however, sought a short cut. They introduced Toy Manchester and, most particularly, Chihuahua blood into their breeding programs, in order to quickly reduce size. Dedicated breeders were appalled and vigorously fought this effort to modify the breed. Once again, they had the strong backing of the United Kennel Club.

Writing in *Bloodlines*, Violet Rinebold, one of our early breeders, and owner of the first National Grand Champion "PR" Rinebold's Winkie, said, "Some crossed the TFT with the Chihuahua or Black and Tan Terrier. Those crossed with the Chihuahua were easy to pick out since they had bowed front legs, more of an apple head... and the tail set was too low."

Dr. E. G. Fuhrman was quite outspoken in denouncing this practice. In 1959, he warned, "The Toy Fox Terrier Associations... the National Association and the U.K.C Registration Office are combining their efforts to keep the Toy Fox Terrier bloodline pure. We are watching for the injection of blood of any other breed in the Toy Fox Terrier..., particularly Chihuahua blood... It is time that this type of breeding was immediately stopped..."

With the continued commitment of dedicated breeders and the strong support of the United Kennel Club, those who sought to cross the Toy Fox Terrier with other breeds were defeated. On August 31, 1960, the United Kennel Club officially closed the stud file on the Toy Fox Terrier. Those days are, thankfully, far behind us. We all owe a debt of gratitude to those hardworking breed pioneers. Thanks to them, today's TFT bloodlines are pure.

FORMATION OF THE NATIONAL AND STATE CLUBS

A dramatic step toward breed progress was taken in the 1940's. Dr. E. G. Fuhrman proposed the formation of a club devoted specifically to the breed. His idea met with an enthusiastic response and, on August 13, 1949, a small band of fanciers assembled at the Hotel Phoenix, in Findlay, Ohio, to discuss the proposal. Dr. Fuhrman came prepared with a sample constitution and by-laws. With the adoption of these documents, the National Toy Fox Terrier Association was officially born. The early breeders attending this first meeting were: Mr. & Mrs. W. W. Bird, Findlay, OH; Mr. & Mrs. John F. Buchman, Tiffin, OH; Mr. & Mrs. Charles L. Dosher, Carmi, IL; Mr. & Mrs. Frank Jones, Aurora, IL; Mr. & Mrs. F. J. Kempher, Van Buren, OH; Mr. & Mrs. A. C. Lanich, Greenville, OH; Mr. & Mrs., Russell E. Mills, New Madison, OH; Mr. & Mrs. Carl V. Rinebold, Fostoria, OH: Mr. & Mrs. Neil Strole, Terre Haute, IN; and Mr. & Mrs. Robert Williams, Leipsic, OH.

Though this group was small, they were all committed to the breed and their enthusiasm was great. The following officers were elected to serve for 1949 – 1950: President—Mr. John F. Buchman; Vice President—Mr. Charles L. Dosher; Secretary/Treasurer—Mr. Neil Strole; and Publicity Director—Mr. Frank Jones. The following members agreed to serve as Directors: Mr. W. W. Bird, Dr. E. G Fuhrman, Mrs. Bessie Kempher, Mrs. Violet E. Rinebold and Mr. Robert Williams.

The first official show of the National Toy Fox Terrier Association was held on August 19, 1950, in Tiffin, Ohio. The members elected Mr. Herman F. Boes, an experienced TFT breeder, to officiate. He became the very first licensed TFT judge. The show was rather simple by today's standards. Entry feeds were $1.00 for the first entry and fifty cents for each additional entry by the same owner. Carl and Violet Rinebold donated a trophy for the Best of Show and Dr. E. G. Fuhrman contributed two engraved silver trays to be awarded to the Best Male and Best Female of Show. Ribbons were presented to the other class winners. This show was a learning experience for all involved. Most had never been in a show ring before and had to learn what was expected. Many people attended merely to observe.

At this first NTFTA show, "PR" Rinebold's Winkie was awarded Best in Show. He was ten months of age and weighed four and a half pounds. He won two more Best in Shows and became the first Toy Fox Terrier champion in August 1952 in Carmi, Illinois. Winkie competed in the first champion class at the NTFTA show in Warsaw, Indiana in 1954 and defeated six other champions to become the first TFT National Grand Champion. In a letter in 1983, Violet Rinebold wrote, "Winkie was born in a litter of four on November 29, 1949, sired by "PR"

In May, 1973, Mr. Fred Miller had just purchased UKC and visited an Illinois Association show. Dorothea Hope had Best of Breed that day. Carl Rinebold was the judge, his last assignment.

Rinebold's Pal Zap (5 1/2 pounds) and out of Rinebold's Missy (6 pounds). We started breeding him at 8 1/2 months and he sired several champions."

The stage had been set and subsequent shows would draw larger entries. The establishment of the National Club did much to spur interest in the breed. It also helped to educate owners in proper breed type. By 1952, there was sufficient interest for the formation of individual state clubs for the breed. The Ohio and Illinois organizations led the way. Since that time, the state clubs have grown steadily in membership. In addition, the establishment of the state clubs allowed enthusiasts more opportunities to show their dogs.

The Toy Fox Terrier has come a long way since those early days. In 1961, Dr. Fuhrman predicted, "There are many good things ahead for the Toy Fox Terrier breed and breeders and owners of these fine little dogs." We have made dramatic progress and see many excellent dogs in the show ring today. With continued effort on the part of all breeders and owners, the Toy Fox Terrier will remain one of the most distinctive and desirable of the toy breeds.

Formation of the American Toy Fox Terrier Club

Breeders of Toy Fox Terriers had long sought recognition by the American Kennel Club. Recognition by AKC is not only a hallmark of honor for every dog breed, but it also allows access to hundreds of shows and trials held across the U.S. For years fanciers considered seeking AKC recognition and some made attempts with no success. Eliza Hopkins wrote the American Kennel Club in July, 1970, asking if the Toy Fox Terrier could be allowed registration in AKC as well as UKC. William F. Stifel, AKC Executive Secretary, responded, "This breed has been registered by the United Kennel Club for many years, and I very frankly can see no possibility at all of our taking on the keeping of the stud book records for the breed at any time in the foreseeable future."

Ten years later, John Davidson inquired what obstacles might stand in the way of AKC recognition of the Toy Fox Terrier. Mark T. Mooty, secretary of AKC, wrote back in January 1980 and repeated Mr. Stifel's words from above, verbatim. He did add, "The fact that the United Kennel provides fanciers of the breed the opportunity for registration and an outlet for competition would seem sufficient." Davidson applied for an Indefinite Listing Privilege in 1981 to compete in obedience, but was denied.

Fourteen years more would pass before significant movement toward AKC recognition would begin. Chrystyne Gettman had shown Chinese Cresteds, Chihuahuas, Min Pins and a Papillon in AKC when she fell in love with Toy Fox Terriers. Although she enjoyed UKC shows, she yearned for the opportunity to show in groups and for Best in Show. She also wanted to be able to have more opportunities to show at venues closer to home. She lamented to her friend, Bill Braun, an AKC delegate and judge, that it seemed TFTs would never be recognized by AKC. Chrystyne says, "Bill returned from a delegates' meeting and called me. He told me it was unanimous among the delegates—AKC wanted us if we really wanted them." Chrystyne began the task of contacting breeders to organize a breed club that would lead the march to AKC recognition.

The American Toy Fox Terrier Club was formed in 1994. The first meeting was held at the home of Frances Macomber in Yakima, Washington. At that time the founding officers and board members were elected. This first board included: Chrystyne Gettman, President; Megan Keefe, Vice President; Joyce Young, Secretary; Diana Morse, Treasurer; Board members Bonita Davis, Dorothy Jacobs, Julie Wells, and Shirley Stroud; Thomas Morse, AKC Delegate. The ATFTC quickly ratified a constitution, by-laws, and a breed standard in 1994. Diana Morse served as registrar for the breed during its first year, receiving and documenting over 200 applications with pedigrees. "Diana took on the job of registration—a huge job and one she should absolutely be given credit for undertaking," says Gettman, the first president. In 1995 the Foundation Stock Service would supplant the need for a club registrar and serve as guardian for the club's stud book during the recognition process. President Gettman was responsible for writing the first standard, communicating with AKC, creating the first website and logo, and writing the first newsletter.

There have been numerous changes in the ATFTC board over the past ten years. One constant has been the steady leadership of Mike Massey as president for six years, both preceding recognition of the breed and during the formative first years as a fully accredited organization. Of his years as president, Massey says, "I make no claim to being knowledgeable about breeding, exhibiting, agility, etc. I know a little more about rescue because all three of my TFTs have been rescued. Any significant decisions that required knowledge from the experts were made by experts from those interests. My role was merely to facilitate their efforts by presiding over the board activities that eventually forged those decisions. I'm a retired fire chief, not an expert on dogs. But I had some experience with organizational dynamics, and that seemed to help."

In July, 2000, the Toy Fox Terrier was moved to the Miscellaneous Class as a precursor to full recognition. During this period, interest and involvement in AKC activities were evaluated prior to final acceptance. The Toy Fox Terrier was officially recognized to compete for championship points in 2003. Since that time there have been four seminal events—the first all-breed Best in Show, the first Champion, the first Best of Breed at Westminster, and the first Eukanuba Best of Breed.

CH. Weeones Hopscotch of Wilkins (Hop)—First Best in Show.

Michele Gauthier will always remember a fateful phone call from Linda Wilkins. Linda called to say she had some very nice puppies for Michele. There was a tricolor female and male—the male was Hop. Her life would never be the same!

Michele says of Hop, "As a puppy Hop thought himself lovely. In fact, he was quite a clown and a show off. I started training him for conformation and it was a piece of cake for him, as he walked right into a stack and was more than happy to

CH. Weeones Hopscotch of Wilkins owned by Michele Gauthier. Judge: Dorothy Nickles. Handler: Wally Rice.

show himself." While Hop was in training, his sister was being shown and won several Best of Breeds in UKC. Then it was Hop's turn.

Recognizing that Hop was not only lovely, but also structurally sound, Michele enlisted the services of professional handler Wally Rice. Wally got on so well with Hop that he finished his AKC championship in three weeks. Then in February he won his first Toy Group and Best in Show at the South Arkansas Kennel Club show under Judge Dorothy Nickles. Hysterical is the only way Michele can describe the phone call from Wally's wife, Carol, announcing the win. Michele remembers, "It was a wonderful thrill for me. There are not words to describe it, except it was the culmination of a dream that started when I was a child."

Hop continued to win and place in groups. He was honored with Best of Breed over 54 entries at the American Toy Fox Terrier National Specialty in Oklahoma City under Judge Laura Perkinson, in May 2003. Again Michele was ecstatic. Another of her dreams had come true! With great humility, Michele admits, "I would like to say that there was this tremendous planning behind Hop's career, but there was not. It simply amounted to the fact I thought he was a good dog and I sent him out and he won and he won."

Michele retired Hop in June, 2003 in conformation and began his training in obedience. He is also producing puppies with which Michele is very satisfied. So if Michele should happen to call you and indicate she has some lovely puppies, you may want to jet down to Ringgold, Louisiana, looking for another Hop!

CH. Valcopy Butch Cassidy (Butchie)—First BB Westminster

Dana Plonkey, breeder/owner of Butchie, refers to him as his Boy Wonder. Butchie's young life has been a succession of firsts. On January 11, 2003, he became the first AKC Toy Fox Terrier to place in a Toy Group. He was only three days beyond his six-month birthday. In eight more days, he would complete his AKC championship with three five-point majors. He was the first male champion of the breed. At ten months of age, he was selected for the first award of merit at the American Toy Fox Terrier Club National specialty. In 2004 he went on to win the coveted first Toy Fox Terrier Best of Breed at the Westminster Kennel Club in New York City.

Butch Cassidy has become the number one Toy Fox Terrier in the country during the first two years of AKC recognition. He has accumulated seventy-nine best of breeds and nineteen group placements. This amazing record has been amassed in limited showing in his own region by his owner/handler. In the ring his records have become the stuff of legends. However, out of the ring, he is an influential sire. Thus far, Butchie has produced several champions, with more nearing titles.

Dana Plonkey remembers Butchie as a puppy, "He was, as the saying goes, a born show dog. At eight weeks, he took to the leash like a natural and at three

CH. Valcopy Butch Cassidy. Judge: Richard Baner. Owner: Dana Plonkey.

months old, his first time out, he went Best in Match at an all toy breed match. From then on there was no stopping him." But his win record and stud records are no more important than his sparkling personality. Butchie feels everyone he meets is special. He may be a boy wonder, but it is no wonder that Dana loves him as he does, "Win or lose, Butchie's personality never changes. He is happy to be out there showing off and making new friends when and where ever he can. His special outgoing and loving temperament is what endears him to everyone he meets, and we feel so lucky, and blessed, to have him as a part of our lives."

CH. Merrylegs' The Mischief Maker (Mindy)—First AKC Champion

Susan McCoy will never forget the day she met Mindy. Susan, who lives in Southern California, had arranged to meet her friend, Megan Keefe, who lives in Northern California, halfway between their respective homes. Megan had a promising nine week old puppy that she had received in return for a stud service and she knew Susan would show her, if she were good enough. Susan recalls, "We met in the pouring rain in a service station parking lot. I, of course, wanted to see what this baby looked like and as there was no shelter to be found; Megan set her down on the sidewalk for just a moment. Although her ears were not up all the way, Mindy stacked herself and looked up at me as if to say, 'Now what?' That was the beginning."

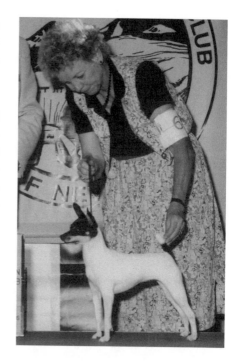

*CH. Merrylegs' The Mischief Maker.
Handler: Bergit Kabel. Photo by Rich
Bergman.*

Mindy loved to show and Susan loved to show her. They adored one another. Showing in the Miscellaneous Class prior to full recognition in 2003, Mindy was a consistent first place winner at Southern California shows. She repeatedly defeated Black Russian Terriers, Glen of Imaal Terriers, and Beaucerons, to take the blue ribbon. She won Best Puppy in Sweepstakes at the ATFTC National Specialty Match at the DelValle, CA show and then went on to take first in the Miscellaneous Class.

On January 1, 2003, the Toy Fox Terrier became eligible to compete for championship points. Mindy and Susan attended the Palm Springs Kennel Club and Toy Breeders of Southern California shows on January 3rd, 4th, and 5th. Mindy was Winners Bitch at all three shows, winning three 5-point majors. Mindy had made history as the first AKC Champion!

This would be Mindy's year as she finished 2003 with 45 Bests of Breed and numerous Toy Group placements. She was the top winning female Toy Fox Terrier for 2003. That year is forever alive in Susan McCoy's memory, "I feel blessed to have had the experience of showing this wonderful little dog and from that first day in the rain, she made my dreams come true."

AKC CH UKC GRCH *Jacobs' I'm Too Sexy For My Fur*
First Eukanuba Best Of Breed

Like so many of today's exhibitors, Dorothy Fisher was bitten by the show bug while showing Anny, her pet TFT. Now Anny is a great pet, but not necessarily a show dog. Only Dot Jacobs could deliver such news without turning off a novice exhibitor, advising Dorothy that she needed a showier specimen. Dorothy was concerned that with her space considerations and work schedule, she could not care for several TFTs. She told Dot that if she purchased a show dog it better be a show stopper because she could not maintain a kennel of TFTs!

AKC CH. UKC GRCH Jacobs' I'm too Sexy For My Fur. Damara Bolté, handler. Photo by Perry Phillips.

Dot surely found that show stopper, as Dorothy fell in love with Fidget the first time she laid eyes on her at a show in Mississippi. So it was that Ms. Fisher found herself flying first class to Florida to pick up Fidget on the Friday before Christmas, 2000. How does a puppy who is too sexy for her fur become Fidget? Well, Fidget has a spunky, tail always up personality. She was always aggravating the other puppies, most of whom were bigger, and she was never in one spot very long—thus, the name! For a five-pound dog, she had a voracious appetite. Once when Dorothy left her motel room for dinner, Fidget unzipped a bag, took out the kibble in a plastic bag, tore into it and had a feast. Need less to say, Fidget looked a little stuffed when she competed in the next day's show!

Fidget WAS a show dog. Dorothy campaigned her to Top Ten status in both registries. Fidget amassed more Top Ten points in 2002 UKC shows than any TFT before or since and she was the UKC Top Ten Breed winner in 2003. One weekend in Georgia, she was BB and BIS in all three UKC shows. Sweeter still was the fact that Dot Jacobs was also there to witness Fidget's wins.

Working five days and showing two days was overwhelming Dorothy. Therefore, after Fidget took her first group placement under Judge Mrs. Ann D. Hearn on July 4, 2003, Dorothy turned Fidget over to Damara Bolte, a successful professional handler. Fidget continued her winning ways, but Dorothy still had not planned to fly Fidget across country to Long Beach, CA in December 2003 for the Eukanuba Invitational. However, with Dot Jacobs' encouragement and the consent of handler, Damara Bolte, Fidget made that momentous flight to California.

Alas, Dorothy's heavy work schedule at the Pentagon precluded her from attending the show. Dorothy's co-workers were aware the morning of the show that Fidget was competing. They watched the clock and waited. Then Dorothy received a call from Damara that Fidget was chosen by Dr. Robert Smith for Best of Breed.

Longtime UKC Breeder Bernice McDermitt in 1994 when she finished 17 Champions. Her kennel produced 240 Champions, Grand Champions and National Grand Champions.

Amidst the congratulations in her office, Dorothy called Dot Jacobs and the shouts of joy in Florida mingled with those in Washington, D.C. Perhaps a little bittersweet for both was the fact that they were not there personally to witness the win and congratulate Fidget and Damara.

Fidget has gone on to be a successful dam for Dorothy, but motherhood finds her still very much a Fidget. Dorothy, who was concerned about caring for multiple dogs, now has a third girl out showing successfully with Damara. One wonders whether Dorothy Fisher will ever hesitate to enter Eukanuba again!

Shirley Thompson, John Davidson and Eliza Hopkins at the 50th Anniversary of The National Toy Fox Terrier Association. Thompson (Toy Acres) and Hopkins bloodlines are behind many of today's winners.

TFT CHARACTER

 The Toy Fox Terrier is a big dog in a little package. Though tiny, in comparison to other breeds, the TFT has the heart of a lion. The late dog writer and judge, Vincent Perry, once wrote that toy dogs "can have the courage of a Marine and the spirit of a tiger." Toy Fox Terrier breeders would certainly concur. The TFT is a combination of two great groups of dogs—the terriers and the toys. As such, he shares characteristics with both groups. Both have influenced his personality and character, and both of these components should be understood and appreciated by those who wish to own a TFT. Early breeders wished to capture the attributes of the Smooth Fox Terrier and condense them into a miniature version. They were eminently successful. The Toy Fox Terrier displays the keen intelligence, courage and animation that is the hallmark of all terriers. These are combined with the quintessential feature of all toy breeds— small size, devotion and an endless, abiding love for their masters.

The Toy Fox Terrier is a versatile little dog. Indeed, it's this versatility that enables the breed to be appreciated on so many levels by such a variety of people. The TFT's small size makes him an ideal choice for people living in apartments, mobile homes or congested cities. Since he doesn't eat much, the TFT is an economical pet for senior citizens or families on limited budgets. With his terrier qualities, the TFT is also well suited to country locales. Many a TFT owner has discovered that his little dog is quite adept at catching mice and rats. Sportsmen have found that the Toy Fox Terrier makes a darn good squirrel dog, and some have even employed the little wonders on larger game. TFTs have a particularly acute sense of hearing and are unfailingly alert. These qualities make the breed an ideal watchdog. As companions, Toy Fox Terriers are the most wonderful little charmers. There's no denying the fact that they are both cute and amusing. It's no wonder that so many people who've been raised with the breed feel their family just isn't complete without a Toy Fox Terrier.

Most Toy Fox Terriers are purchased as companions. It's amazing how quickly they become full-fledged members of the family. They adore living in the midst

TFT's are ideal companions. "PR" Meadowood's Jillian and "PR" Casas Adobe's Amber keep Judy Guillot, of Tucson, Arizona, company. Photo by David Ring.

of all the day-to-day goings on and they want to be a part of it all. TFTs become very attached to their families and often demand to be included in all activities. So closely do they identify with the family, sometimes one wonders if a TFT even realizes that he's a dog! It is the breed's quick intelligence that wins the Toy Fox Terrier so many admirers. Nowhere is this more apparent than with the house dog. Since he bonds so intimately with the family, your Toy Fox Terrier will learn to read you. Experts tell us that dogs respond more to tone of voice than to words. However, you'll quickly learn that your TFT has learned to recognize certain words and clearly understands their meaning. Say "walk" and you'll find your dog waiting for you at the door. Most Toy Fox Terriers enjoy riding in the car. The minute he hears the word, he'll probably jump up excitedly, eager to go along. Some owners have tried spelling out the letters "c-a-r," in an attempt to fool their dogs. The Toy Fox Terrier, however, quickly figures out this ruse.

Like all toy dogs, the Toy Fox Terrier readily adapts to the ways of your family. If your household tends to be noisy and excitable, your dog is apt to be noisy, too. In a relaxed and quiet household, chances are the dog will respond in a similar fashion. One must realize, however, that with his terrier background, the Toy Fox Terrier is an animated, energetic dog. Those looking for a very quiet, mellow dog would be happier with a less dynamic breed.

Be forewarned, your Toy Fox Terrier will think he should share everything in your life. Typically, he'll prefer to sleep on your bed. If you have a midnight snack, your TFT will think he's entitled, too. You'll discover that he has abundant intelligence and is eager to please. At the same time, however, you'll learn that he has a mind of his own. He will probably challenge you to see just what he can get away with. You'll have to discipline him. Even so, you may wonder, after a time, if you own your Toy Fox Terrier or if it's the other way around!

Very often, Toy Fox Terriers become one-person or one-family dogs. Some dogs seem to have the same degree of love and devotion for the entire family. However, it's not unusual for a TFT to single out one family member as his one special person. Indeed, most Toy Fox Terriers become intensely loyal. For this reason, your dog may not respond eagerly to strangers. While some dogs will greet visitors enthusiastically, others don't care about anyone but their owners. Many TFTs simply won't lavish affection on a person they don't know. You should train your dog to accept visitors admitted to your home. After all, you do want him to act properly. However, it may be best for the visitor to wait for the dog to make the approach, rather than forcing the contact. Many Toy Fox Terriers like to stand back and size up people before coming to them. As long as the visitors act properly themselves, all will go well. However, let them do something that the dog considers improper, and your TFT is likely to raise a ruckus.

The Toy Fox Terrier may be a toy dog, but you'll never convince him of that! No sissy is he. There's not one fearful bone in that little body. Because of this, TFT owners have to exercise a

Good Family Pets.
Morgan and Lily Van Allen of
Hudson, WI.

degree of caution with their dogs. The Toy Fox, as we have implied, will jealously guard his home and his owners. He won't hesitate to confront larger dogs aggressively. One TFT in Alaska even chased bears away from his yard. Therefore, when you take your dog for a walk, particularly if he might encounter other dogs, it's best to have him on leash. This small measure of protection might well save his life.

This, then, is the Toy Fox Terrier. A gay, amusing charmer who is uncommonly devoted to his owner, be it one person or an entire family. He is bold and self-confident. A Toy Fox Terrier is also proud. With his flashy colors and sleek good looks, he struts around like he's ready to take on the world. He is also an energetic, lively, sparkling toy dog who greets each day with enthusiasm and a zest for living. His cocky, daring manner and deep loyalty is what makes people so fond of the breed. He's an animated bundle of love, with the spirit of a tiger, on four little legs.

As we've said, your Toy Fox Terrier will consider himself a member of the family. He'll consider it his duty, therefore, to protect you from all intruders. With the TFT's keen sense of hearing and his abundant courage, he makes an ideal watchdog. Indeed, he's a four-legged burglar alarm. He'll spring to attention and run to the door the minute he hears a car in the driveway or someone approaching the door. For his size, the TFT has a big bark and he won't stop as long as something is amiss. Many burglars find it far more desirable to rob a house without such a vigilant and noisy alarm.

TFT's owned and loved by Luann Stovall. "Don't leave us behind."

UNDERSTANDING
THE STANDARD

 "The Toy Fox Terrier breed has come a long way…We now have many dogs of good type that are excellent specimens of the breed in every respect. Our shows have been a great means of educating breeders and owners as to type, conformation and color and markings…" Dr. E.G. Fuhrman wrote in 1959. He would doubtless be very pleased with the dogs seen in today's show rings. Through the years, there has been consistent improvement in breed quality. Today's dedicated TFT breeders, through careful planning, have sought to move the breed toward the elusive goal of perfection, as expressed in the standard. As always, much work remains to be done. It is hoped that all breeders will strive to better understand the TFT standard.

A standard can be a confusing and mystifying document for the novice. In truth, the standard is simply a word picture that lists the Toy Fox Terrier's essential characteristics. It delineates those qualities that differentiate the TFT from every other breed and it also provides a guideline for the evaluation of individual dogs. The standard assumes that the reader has a basic knowledge of dogs and their structure. It frequently uses terms that are unknown to the novice.

Standards, by their very nature, are brief. While they may be very explicit on some points, such as color and markings, they can't possibly include all the fine nuances that are difficult to express in words. The standard is also flexible. Certainly the breeder or judge cannot ignore the essentials detailed in the standard. There is, however, room for personal interpretation. The standard allows breeders to express their own interpretations, as long as they vigilantly comply with the basic requirements.

It is essential for every breeder of Toy Fox Terriers to have an intimate understanding of the standard, which serves as the guideline for the breed. It's not enough to simply read the standard or even to memorize it. Instead, you must understand why it is important for the TFT to have those qualities. The successful breeder is one who reads the standard with an analytical eye, trying to decipher not only its words, but also its intent. Novices should study the standard and then view as many TFTs

Ch. "PR" Currens' Nadine of Parkside was owned by Doris and the late Howard Currens. Nadine is a lovely example of the breed. Note her balance and typical keen alertness.

as possible. Don't be afraid to speak to experienced breeders and judges. Once they realize that you have a sincere desire to learn about the breed, they'll be willing to explain their views to you. You'll learn about their personal interpretations and the points that they consider vital in their breeding programs. Their experiences will serve as a guide to obtaining stock and planning your own breeding program.

The AKC and UKC standards are extremely parallel in setting forth the physical attributes of the TFT. The AKC standard may be downloaded from

TOY FOX TERRIER STANDARD

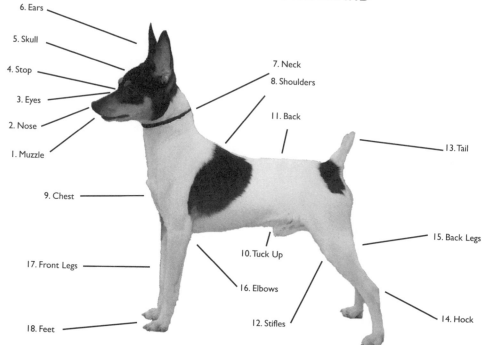

6. Ears
5. Skull
4. Stop
3. Eyes
2. Nose
1. Muzzle
7. Neck
8. Shoulders
11. Back
13. Tail
9. Chest
15. Back Legs
17. Front Legs
10. Tuck Up
16. Elbows
18. Feet
12. Stifles
14. Hock

www.akc.org and the UKC standard from www.ukcdogs.com. These two standards diverge in three important areas—history, size, and color. The differences in heritage will be delineated while size and color will be dealt with later in this chapter.

The UKC standard does not acknowledge that the TFT was mixed with any other breeds, while the AKC standard contends that several breeds were introduced to the lineage of the TFT. The UKC standard asserts that the runts from Smooth Fox Terrier litters were selected as the foundation stock of the TFT. The AKC standard asserts that Smooth Fox Terriers were bred with several toy breeds including the Chihuahua and Manchester Terrier. Old timers in the breed admitted that the Smooth Fox Terrier, as registered with UKC between 1912 and 1936, looked little like the Smooth Fox Terrier of today. In fact, the Smooth Fox Terriers that UKC registered during this period had been more of the farm-type terrier. These terriers were used on farms to control vermin and hunt rabbit and squirrel. These 7 – 10 pound black and white canines were often just called rat terriers. They were more often drop-eared, barrel bodied with short legs, and more black than white, with abundant ticking and typical tan markings. It is likely the smaller puppies from such foundation stock formed the Toy Fox Terrier. It would be difficult to prove just who mixed what with these early terriers. Most veteran breeders believed mixing probably occurred and it is hardly worth debating at this point. It is a distinctive phenotype today and a breed to be truly appreciated regardless of what one believes about its heritage.

1904 Calendar showing typical pet terrier.

GENERAL APPEARANCE

A well-made Toy Fox Terrier is eye catching. He cannot be faked. There is no profuse coat to conceal his true structure. No trimming or brushing will improve the looks nature gave him. While he's a toy and must, therefore, be small, he is also all terrier. He shows the typical, and essential, keen alertness found in all terriers. He's always ready for action, be it a tussle or a romp in the woods. He is full of vim and vigor. Extremely confident, he gives the impression that he's full of himself. Self possessed, he radiates energy combined with elegance, and he's absolutely sure that he's equal to any other dog (humans too, perhaps) regardless of size. He acts, looks and moves like an aristocrat. His short, glossy coat and brilliant, rich coloring give him a flashy appearance. His beauty, however, doesn't depend on mere flashiness. All of his body parts combine harmoniously into a smooth whole. The highly held head, the long, finely arched neck, the compact body and the upright tail join to give him a look of poise and balance. Keenly alert, nimble, quick, small, but powerful and built for great endurance, the Toy Fox Terrier wraps it all up in a svelte, elegant package.

The Head

The Toy Fox Terrier's head is the truest indicator of breed type. A typical head is what stamps the dog unmistakably a TFT. Open a book which features head studies of dogs. As you flip from page to page,

Ch. "PR" Hopkins' Jeff's Janice.

you should be able to identify each and every breed by the appearance of the head. It is likewise true that the TFT's alertness, intelligence and character are most clearly seen in the appearance of his head. In past years, head faults in Toy Fox Terriers were common. Dogs with wide-set, rounded ears, bulging eyes, abrupt stops (defined below) and short muzzles were common in show rings. With dedication and vigilance, breeders have succeeded in minimizing these faults. While these failings still exist, they are rarely seen in today's winners. While the emphasis on head may seem exaggerated, we need to remember that the head is likely to be the first thing seen. The buyer who comes to your house, in search of a pet, will most likely pick a puppy up and look at it's head first. Similarly, as the judge approaches to examine your dog individually in the show ring, the head generally commands his attention first. While it may not seem fair, the dog with a faulty head is likely to be dismissed without a second look. Breeders should avoid, however, becoming obsessed with the head, to the exclusion of the body. A beautiful Toy Fox Terrier

*UKC and AKC CH Dreammer Boy
owned by George and Margi Hill.
Photo by Mary Bloom.*

head should always be balanced and complemented by a good body. Breeders should concentrate on the total dog and not become merely headhunters.

It is vitally important that the head be in proportion to the rest of the body. A large head, no matter how excellent, will look ridiculous on a small body. Likewise, a tiny head perched on a large body looks ludicrous. The head that would be perfect on a seven pound Toy Fox Terrier will completely overwhelm a four pound dog. The head must look as though it fits and belongs on the individual dog.

In addition to being in proportion to the body, the head must be proportional itself. The TFT has a very balanced head. The distance from the occiput (back point of the skull) to the stop (or dividing line between the skull and the muzzle) should equal the distance from the stop to the nose. If these dimensions are unequal, it will mar the head's overall appearance. The best Toy Fox Terrier head will be medium in length and width, with a medium stop.

The Skull

We must, once again, use the words medium or moderate when describing the TFT's skull. A correctly shaped skull is free of exaggeration and should be slightly rounded, rather than flat. The high ear set may give the skull the appearance of flatness, but examination will reveal otherwise. The backskull should be moderate in width. A common fault is too broad a backskull, in which the ears are wide-set. In addition, the shape of the foreskull, or forehead, has a great influence on TFT expression. Any tendency toward a bulging or domed foreskull is a very serious fault, indeed. This irregular roundness of the skull is referred to as an "apple head." Apple heads are severely faulted in the show ring because they destroy true TFT expression. While apple heads may occur in any size TFT, they are more prevalent in very small dogs.

The skull gradually decreases in width to the eyes. The cheeks have a clean-cut leanness. They are relatively flat and muscular, and should not bulge. A Toy Fox Terrier should never look as though he has a chestnut tucked away in his cheeks.

Bulging cheek muscles destroy the lean outline of the muzzle When viewed from the front or in profile, the head can best be described as a blunt wedge. In the words of the UKC standard: "When viewed from the front, the head widens gradually from the black nose to the base of the ears in practically an unbroken line." To assure this look, the area beneath the eyes must be well filled in or the muzzle appears narrow and snipy. While to some novices the short muzzle may appear cute, it is entirely wrong for the breed. Often, the short muzzle is accompanied by the round head and pronounced stop. Being a descendant of the Fox Terrier, it is imperative that the shape of the TFT's muzzle suggests strength. The lips should fully cover the teeth, but there should be no excessive skin. Hanging, pendant lips, or flews, give the TFT a houndy appearance that is totally incorrect. The lips must always be dry, never drooly.

Stop

The stop is the dividing line between the skull and the muzzle. Generally located just below the eye level, it is the point where the nasal bone and the skull meet. The TFT should have a moderate stop. Too little stop will give a sighthound appearance and may be accompanied by a Roman nose. A far more common fault, particularly in tiny Toy Fox Terriers, is too much stop. This pronounced stop is usually accompanied by an overly short muzzle, and the dog may have the undesirable rounded or apple head as well. Too much stop is a fault to be carefully guarded against, for it destroys true TFT expression. A moderate stop can best be explained to mean slightly sloping—a midpoint between the abrupt stop of the Chihuahua and the non-stop of the Collie.

Ears

"We have better heads on our dogs and there are many more dogs that have natural, erect ears. The ears are very important and they should stand erect. We find that we are gradually getting away from the flop-over of the tip of the ear in the Toy Fox Terrier breed," said Dr. E.G. Fuhrman, in 1959. Indeed, breeders have made strong advances in this area in recent years. Like most breeders, I have not had a TFT whose ears were not naturally erect in my 35 years of breeding these little dogs.

While most TFTs have large ears, it is important that the ears be in proportion to the size of the head. The ears should always be strongly erect. The ear leather (the outer cartilage) should be thin, but with enough strength to keep the ears upright. Thick, heavy ears are more likely to lop over or to flop as the TFT moves. The ears should always be pointed in a V-shape, rather than rounded. This upright open ear is less prone to infection than a drop ear.

It is difficult to say when a puppy's ears will come up. Generally, the ears on smaller pups come up more quickly than those on larger pups. Stress can also affect

Ch. "PR" Hopkins' A Mischievous Gretta bred by Eliza Hopkins and co-owned with Deborah Hays. Photo by Cindy K. Rogers.

ear carriage in young TFT puppies. Ears are likely to go up and down during the teething period. Lop or hanging ears are a very serious fault in a mature Toy Fox Terrier. The ears are set rather high on the head. They should, however, not be placed so close together that they touch. The ears must point straight forward so that the entire interior of the ear is visible from the front. The ears should never flare outward or be placed on the side of the head. Ears that are too widely set greatly detract from the TFT's alert expression. Both registries' standards disqualify non-erect ears on TFTs six months or older.

Eyes

It is often said that eyes are the mirror of the soul. Indeed, the TFT's eyes do capture much of the breed's character. Those bright, sparkling eyes convey an impression of intelligence and alertness. They are one of the breed's most endearing and charming traits, and at times they seem almost able to talk. When a TFT is excited, his eyes seem full of fire and intensity. When the dog is relaxed, the Toy Fox Terrier has a kind, gentle expression that can melt the hardest heart.

The ideal Toy Fox Terrier eye is round in shape. The round eye does much to soften the TFT's expression. One does occasionally see eyes that are slightly oval in shape, but they must never be small and squinty. The eyes are to be prominent and well set in the socket. Under no circumstances should the eyes bulge. The bulging eye, which gives a buggy appearance, is most likely to be seen in dogs with the undesirable rounded, apple head. This bulging eye is most common today in very small Toy Fox Terriers.

Although it is not mentioned in the standard, the skin fits tightly around the eye. No portion of the third eyelid, or haw, should be visible. When the haw shows, it gives the TFT a Bloodhound look that is quite untypical of the breed. The area encircling the eye is dry in appearance and should never have a weepy, tearing look.

The eyes should always be very dark in color. Most breeders prefer an eye as close as possible to black. The iris should fill the eye with no white showing. When white is seen in the corners of the eye, the dog has a look of perpetual surprise that detracts from the keen alertness so desired in TFT expression. A reddish-brown eye color can sometimes be seen in white and tan dogs. However, the darker eye is always preferred. The eye rims should always be black in tri-color or white/black's, or tan in white/tan's and white/chocolate's. Flesh colored eye rims, or rims with pink spots, seriously mar the TFT's appearance. Thankfully, this fault is seldom seen.

Nose

The standard calls for a coal black nose. Novices are often astounded when they have their first TFT litter. Newborn pups are born with pink noses that darken as the pups grow. The noses of some pups seem to turn black overnight, while others become spotted or freckled with black. In most cases the nose will be fully black by weaning time. However, pink spots or flesh colored spots are faulted. Many of these spots will fill in as the puppy matures. Even though the muzzle surrounding the nose may be white in color, the nose should still be jet black. Light-colored noses are seldom a problem in TFTs, but they can occur. Occasionally a nose spot or section will darken but the pinkish sheen still can be seen. In the white and tan TFT, liver colored noses are sometimes seen. Liver-colored noses are disqualified in the UKC standard and Dudley noses (flesh-colored) are disqualified in both UKC and AKC standards. In short, any color other than coal black should be faulted in the show ring. The TFT's nostrils should be large and open. Tiny, pinched nostrils, which may impair breathing, will hinder endurance and are atypical and incorrect.

The Bite

Both UKC and AKC standards prescribe the scissors bite. This desired bite, in which the teeth enmesh tightly, with the upper front teeth fitting snugly over the bottom

AKC CH UKC GRCH Chestnut's Miss Congeniality "Gracie" bred by Judy Chestnut Threlfall and owned by Mark and Judy Threlfall. Exhibited by Judy Threlfall.

front teeth, is the strongest type of dental alignment. It allows the dog to grasp an object firmly and hold on. When we remember that, early on, Toy Fox Terriers often dispatched rats in rural barns, we'll be able to see the significance of a good tight scissors bite. Clearly, it takes a good, strong bite to hold a squirming rat.

In addition, the teeth should be strong. The canine teeth, sometimes called the tusks or fangs, should be especially prominent and well formed. Between them sit the six smaller incisor teeth. Ideally, these should sit in a straight line and not be overly crowded. However, in toy dogs, these teeth can sometimes be slightly out of alignment. While this is not the ideal, it should not be faulted if the bite itself is a good scissors fit.

The UKC standard accepts a level bite while the AKC standard does not address it or list it as a fault. In a level bite, the front teeth (the incisors) of the upper and lower jaws meet exactly. While a level bite is certainly preferable to an undershot or overshot bite, it is far less efficient than a scissors bite. Since the upper teeth ride on the lower teeth, as the dog ages, the teeth will erode and wear down. By the time the dog is several years old, all that may remain are shards of the original teeth. As the canine teeth are still in basic alignment, the dog will have more grasping power than with an undershot or overshot bite. However, because the teeth don't hold up as well, the UKC standard gives preference to the more sound scissors bite. Care should be taken when breeding dogs with level bites. Some breeders have discovered that dogs with level bites are more prone to producing undershot bites in subsequent generations.

In the undershot bite, the teeth of the lower jaw project beyond those of the upper jaw. In an extremely pronounced underbite, the teeth may even be visible when the mouth is closed. Many years ago, underbites were a frequently found fault in Toy Fax Terriers. One could sit at ringside and see noticeable underbites. Undershot jaws give the TFT a Bulldog type appearance that is totally foreign to the breed. Since undershot bites are inherited, breeders must take special care to eliminate such dogs from their breeding programs. Puppies with underbites should be sold as pets and registration papers withheld until the breeder receives confirmation that the puppy has been spayed or neutered. An undershot bite is a disqualification in both the UKC and AKC standards.

The overshot bite is the exact opposite of the undershot. In this case, the upper jaw overlaps and does not touch the front teeth of the lower jaw. While overbites are not common in the Toy Fox Terrier, they can occur and should be guarded against. The overshot bite has little power and grasping ability. A dog with an overshot jaw has an uncharacteristically weak expression. When the dog is viewed in profile, the lower jaw appears to lack substance and finish. The AKC standard provides for a disqualification for overbites of more than 1/8th inch while UKC standard faults an overbite of 1/16th inch and disqualifies 1/8th inch.

When evaluating the bites on puppies, beware of disregarding a pup with a slight overbite. The lower jaw grows out more slowly than the upper jaw and in most cases, as the puppy matures, the bite will develop into a proper scissors bite. A pronounced overbite, however, is not likely to correct with time. Undershot bites seldom, if ever, correct as the puppy grows.

Frequently, toy dogs are slow to lose their baby teeth. Therefore, it's not uncommon to see a young dog with a double row of teeth. Generally, the puppy teeth loosen and fall out before six months of age. However, some teeth stubbornly remain in place. While some veterinarians will remove these extra teeth, others prefer to wait until the dog reaches six months of age. Since it's often necessary to anesthetize the dog to remove the teeth, many vets feel it is risky to perform this operation on a young pup. Some judges find these double teeth objectionable. However, if the bite is in proper scissors alignment, the dog should not be penalized until one year of age, according to the UKC standard.

Occasionally, a Toy Fox Terrier may have lost a tooth or two. Since the TFT's mouth is so small, special care must be taken in keeping the teeth clean and free of tartar. Without such care, the TFT may well lose some of his teeth. However, teeth can be lost in other ways, too. Some TFTs are accomplished jumpers and climbers. Indeed, some Toy Fox Terriers act as though they are part mountain goat. An accidental spill may cause a TFT to lose a tooth. A fight between two TFTs can also result in the loss of a tooth. Once again, if the jaw is properly aligned, this should not be a cause for faulting an otherwise good dog. Both UKC and AKC standards agree that as long as the bite can be determined, loss of teeth should not be faulted.

Head Color and Markings

The AKC and UKC standards clearly describe the color and markings to be found on the Toy Fox Terrier's head. In all color varieties, white is NOT to be predominate on the head. The head color should be predominately black, tan, or chocolate with the colored areas free of white or brown hairs.

The tri-colored TFT has tan trim over the eyes and on the cheeks and muzzle. The tan over the eyes appears as small dots or seeds of color. These should be distinctly tan, without interspersed black hairs. The amount of tan trim on the cheeks and muzzle varies from dog to dog. The color of the trim may vary from a light flaxen to a rich, clear tan. Most breeders and judges prefer the brilliant rich tan that makes such a lovely accent. Some breeders describe this rich tan as mahogany in color. In newborns, the tan markings on the head are truly tiny. However, they grow in size as the pups develop and by weaning time, you will clearly see if the desired markings are present. White frost or tiny white spots on the lower muzzle and surrounding the nose are acceptable.

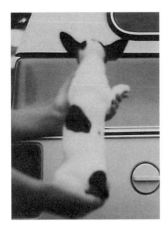

The white on the back of this puppy's head actually touches the ears.

The ears on the white, black, and tan and the black and white TFT should be black on the backside. An outline or edging of black should rim the inner edge, or front part, of the ear. Some tan hairs may mingle with the black on the back of the ears, but the overall color should be definitely black. Likewise, a few tan hairs may appear at the base of the insides of the ears. White on the back of the ears or any white shading should be avoided.

White, chocolate and tan (AKC only) and white and tan TFTs will have the same distribution of chocolate or tan on the head and ears as the black in the tricolor described above. Some white and tans may have a lighter or darker shade of tan as trim on the cheeks, muzzle or eye dots. This trim may not be apparent on other white and tans. Chocolates will have sharply defined tan on the cheeks, muzzle and eye dots. Both white and tans and white, chocolate and tans may have white frosting or small white spots on the lower muzzle.

Blazes

The TFT is permitted to have a white blaze. A blaze is a white strip running down the face, between the eyes. Some breeders prefer dogs without blazes. Blazes

can make a visual difference in the appearance of the head. The all black head gives the muzzle a shorter appearance, while a white blaze causes the muzzle to appear somewhat longer. The blaze should never be so wide that it touches the eyes or ears. Such a blaze would result in a disqualification in the AKC show ring and would be faulted in UKC. Breeders prefer a symmetrical, properly centered blaze. Off-center blazes are acceptable, however, and should not be penalized, as long as they are not wide enough to touch the eyes.

This puppy's blaze is too wide. Note that it touches the eye.

Body

A well-balanced look is essential to a good Toy Fox Terrier. In general type, the TFT has a square look. The height from the bottom of the feet to the withers (highest point of the shoulders) should appear approximately equal to the length from the point

Ch. "PR" Hopkins' Jeff's Janice, owned by Hopkins Kennel, illustrates the correct, strong topline.

of the shoulder to the point of the rump. Breeders must always strive for moderation and balance. Many years ago, we saw varying body types in the breed. Overly cobby dogs with broad chests, short legs and no tuck up were common. They might be standing next to a dog of the deer type, who was overly tall, with spindly bone, a narrow chest, long body and exaggerated tuck up. Thankfully, we rarely see such extremes any more. A beautifully proportioned Toy Fox Terrier, who at the same time embodies strength and elegance, is what we strive for today.

Some variation is still seen in body length. A too short back, although rare, makes the body appear chunky. This is most undesirable, as it gives the dog a sausage-like appearance. More common is the longer body. Dogs with longer bodies often lack width, which destroys the desired strong appearance. Some breeders are apt to allow a little more body length in a bitch, in the belief that it will give her more room to carry puppies. However, if her body length is such that it detracts from the square appearance, she should be faulted.

The Toy Fox Terrier's amount of bone and length of leg should also be proportional and balanced. A short, stocky body supported on short, sturdy legs is not pleasing to the eye. The legs must be proportionate, to correctly balance and carry the body. The Toy Fox Terrier should have a moderate amount of bone. Heavily boned dogs do occur, but are not common. You're more likely to see a dog with insufficient, spindly bone. TFT puppies often appear to have somewhat heavier bone when they are young. The bone will consolidate and be proper as the puppy grows. Beware of the puppy that seems to have slight bone when he's young. Almost always, he'll be too finely boned when he matures.

Forequarters

The forequarters, or front assembly, is the most difficult part of the body to understand and explain. The neck, shoulders, ribs, chest and front legs are all interrelated. If one of these individual parts is faulty, it tends to throw the whole front assembly out of kilter. It is for this reason that faults in the forequarters are the most difficult to eradicate from a breeding program. While a poor rear may often be corrected in a

This female has an extremely faulty front. This is a classic example of a dog that is "out at the elbows." In addition, her ears are set too wide and flair out to the side. If you look closely, you'll also see that her tail was docked too long.

single generation, faults of the front assembly often take many breedings to correct. It takes careful study, evaluation and comparison of dogs to understand fully the requirements for a properly proportioned and angulated front assembly. Faults in the forequarters often show up in motion. We'll take each of the parts of the forequarters in order and attempt to explain their relationship to each other.

Neck

The neck is something more than a mere support for the head. The neck should be clean, muscular and rather long. There should be a slight arch. The elegant, strong neck is very important in the TFT. The length of the neck should approximate the length of the head. We must remember that, in the past, the Toy Fox Terrier was used for ratting. He had to have ample length of neck to quickly grab the rat, without lowering his body. He also needed sufficient strength to shake his head from side to side, breaking the rat's neck. This takes flexibility and power. While your TFT isn't likely to be employed as a rat catcher today, you will often see him take one of his toys and shake it in a similar manner.

The neck should be clean, without excessive throatiness. There should be no hanging folds of extra skin. Thin, spindly necks lack power and should be faulted. Similarly, short heavy necks, where the head appears to perch on the shoulders, detract from the TFT's appearance and are structurally

Gr CH Dominos Super Star John Davidson's First Champion. Note the lovely flowing lines, as the neck blends into the shoullder blades and cleanly melds into the topline. In addition, this dog's front and rear angluation match perfectly, giving him a well balanced look.

incorrect. The neck should have a slight arch. Rigidly straight necks, which lack flexibility, should be faulted. Also the concave, or ewe-neck, is a serious fault and is usually accompanied by a too straight shoulder. With the desired slight arch, the Toy Fox Terrier holds his head high and shows the alert confidence that's so typical of the breed.

The neck should widen gradually to the shoulders. An elegant neck blends smoothly into well-laid back shoulders. It should be noted that there are the same number of vertebrae in the neck of a dog that appears short necked as in one with the correct length. The position of the shoulder blades and their degree of angulation contribute visibly to the appearance of neck length. The neck on a dog with steep, upright shoulders begins further up the vertebrae than the dog with properly sloping shoulders. This creates a short-necked look. An elegant neckline, which slopes smoothly into properly placed shoulders, makes for a stylish appearance in the show ring and greatly enhances your TFT's appearance.

Shoulders

The shoulders should be long, sloping and laid back at a 45-degree angle. This degree of slope to the shoulder is 2 1/2 times more efficient that a 60-degree slope in lifting the front legs. The should blade (scapula) should be about the same length as the humerus (upper front leg bone) and form a 90 degree angle where they meet.

When you feel the withers (highest point of the shoulders) you should be able to tell that the shoulder blades are placed close together. Look at the dog in profile. If you see one smooth, continuous line extending from the neck, past the shoulder blades, without a rise or dip, the dog most likely has very good shoulders. There should never be an abrupt break where the neck and the shoulders join. Similarly, a dip in the back, behind the shoulder blades, usually indicates insufficient layback. The ideal shoulder layback allows the dog to extend his front legs with maximum reach. When viewed from the side, the legs should swing freely in a straight line from the shoulders. (i.e., there should be no break at the elbow or foot). Straight shoulders are seen fairly often in Toy Fox Terriers, and breeders should strive for better, more correct layback.

An extremely poor TFT, with more faults than you can count. Note the very wide facial blaze. The dog lacks overall balance and appears rangy. He does not have sufficient depth or width of chest, and appears to be perched on stilts.

Nat. Gr. Ch. "PR" Gorden's Toy Rooster, owned by Doug and Betty Gorden, of Crosby, Texas, shows a correct front assembly. Note the straight front, good width of chest and proper length of neck.

Chest and Ribs

The Toy Fox Terrier has a deep chest and well-defined ribs. When viewed from the side, the brisket (forepart of the chest) should extend to or just above the elbow. A TFT with inadequate depth of brisket appears to be unduly leggy, as though he was perched on stilts. When viewed from the front, the chest should be wide enough to enable the legs to stand parallel to each other.

The well-sprung rib cage is neither too narrow (slab-sided) nor too wide (barrel-shaped). The proper oval-shaped rib cage greatly enhances endurance, a key characteristic of the Toy Fox Terrier. The circumference of the chest will narrow somewhat behind the elbows. This allows the dog clearance in bringing his front legs back. The barrel-chest cannot expand as freely when the dog exerts himself. This fault is often accompanied by an overly wide, Bulldog-like chest. In motion, the barrel-chested dog cannot get his front legs back behind him. Instead, they hit the chest and cause interference. In order to avoid this, the elbows are often forced out. Barrel-chested dogs usually have too much width between the tops of the shoulder blades. The slab-sided dog is apt to be short on endurance, too. The lungs, contained in the rib cage, must be able to expand as the dog runs. If there's not enough room for this to occur, endurance will be hampered.

Front Legs

The front legs should drop straight from the elbows to the feet. They should be the same distance apart at the elbow as at the feet. For this to happen, the chest must be moderately wide. When the chest is too wide, the legs are usually forced out at the elbows. This fault gives a very coarse, clumsy, Bulldog-like appearance and is to be heavily penalized. A too narrow chest allows the dog to bring his elbows together under his body. This, too, should be faulted in the show ring. French fronts, Chippendale fronts or east-west fronts occur when the legs turn outward below the pasterns. This loose, unsound front is often found and should be faulted.

The old style TFT was overly broad and coarse, and frequently was out at the elbows. While breeders have greatly reduced these faults, they can still be found and should be penalized.

The pasterns should appear straight, strong and flexible. They should be nearly perpendicular to the ground. There is actually a very slight (20-degree) slope to the pasterns, which helps cushion the feet and absorb shock. There should be a slight 'give' or springiness to the pasterns, but they must, under no circumstances, be sloped. This is called 'down in the pasterns' and is a serious and ugly fault.

Feet

People often make the mistake of overlooking the feet. However, poor feet can spoil the TFT's overall appearance. Large, splayed, or thin feet will mar the look of the most beautiful dog. Good feet are also more functional. Being a long lived and active breed, it is important that the feet hold up throughout the dog's lifetime.

Toy Fox Terriers have hare feet. In this type of foot, the two middle toes are longer than the outside toes. The feet should be compact. Splayed feet, in which the toes spread, are apt to be faulted in the show ring, although not specifically identified as a fault in the standard. Proper care of the nails will help to prevent splaying. When nails become overly long, they cause the toes to spread. The pads should be thick enough to cushion the feet and absorb shock.

The TFT always has dewclaws on the front legs and may have them on the rear legs. Even though the standard makes no mention of the dewclaws, most breeders remove them to improve appearance and to avoid possible injury.

Underline

The Toy Fox Terrier's belly should be moderately tucked up. This gentle rise contributes much to the appearance of elegance and agility. An extreme tuck up is incorrect, however. Too much tuck up gives a Greyhound appearance. It is generally coupled with an arch or roach of the loin and, often, with a low tail set. This is clearly at odds with the strong, level back called for in the standard.

Hindquarters

The Toy Fox Terrier has a strong and muscular rear. For his size, he is quite strong. The upper thighs are quite powerful. They are broad and muscular but not beefy. Excessively muscled thighs appear coarse and bunchy. When viewed from behind, the legs, hocks, and feet should be straight. The point of the hock should be close to the ground and strong. The hind pastern must always be perfectly upright. Hocks and pasterns should point neither in nor out. Cowhocks, in which the hocks turn inward toward each other, is a common fault and should be severely penalized in the show ring. Hocks which turn outward are barrel-hocked and move wide with a waddle. The hock joint may be 130 – 140 degrees to produce a smooth trotting gait. The more let down, or close to ground, the hock joint the better.

The pelvic bone slopes at about 30-degrees off the horizontal. This allows for maximum backreach. A dog that moves with short, choppy steps probably has too steep a pelvis for speed and endurance. The femur, or thighbone, attaches at approximately 90-degrees to the line of the pelvis. It should be noted that balance between front and rear assemblies is best when the 90-degree angle is present fore and aft. Most breeders and judges agree that the TFT has a moderate bend of stifle when viewed from the side. Since the rear is the source of the dog's drive and power when moving, moderate angulation allows the dog to step out with a free and easy stride. The overly angulated rear often tends to be weaker and gives the dog a crouched appearance in the rear. Straight stifles are equally faulty for they restrict the dog's movement. The straight-stifled dog moves with a stilted, stick-like action. Sometimes it can be difficult for the judge to accurately gauge the bend of stifle in the Toy Fox Terrier. Many an adequately angulated TFT will tense his muscles when posed in the show ring, giving the appearance of being straight–stifled. Dogs that are particularly showy and keyed up in the ring often display this tenseness. In such cases, the judge should try to catch the dog in a more relaxed moment and pay close attention when he gaits.

Tail

Next to the head, the tail is the most expressive part of the Toy Fox Terrier. That little stub of a tail has a language all its own. An upright tail bespeaks a bold, confident and alert nature. Although a TFT may drop his tail at ease, a TFT with his tail glued to his bottom looks as though he is cringing, fearful or not feeling well. The Toy Fox Terrier is a cocky little breed and his upright tail demonstrates his innate self-confidence and sense of importance. A TFT who carries his tail low appears shy and fearful.

Gr. Ch. "PR" Byrd's Mi-Treasure, owned by Ronald and Colleen Byrd, of Berger, Missouri, a lovely TFT. Although one of her rear legs is extended farther back than normal, you can still see the appearance of strength.

The tail must be set very high. It should be directly on the level of the back and carried upright. The set-on of the tail is very important. While a TFT's show ring appearance may be marred by an incorrectly docked tail, an improper tail-set may be passed on to the next generation. The tail is an extension of the back's vertebrae. When a TFT has a low-set tail, the back has a squatty, roach-like appearance and may appear longer. In motion, the Toy Fox should carry his tail bolt upright. Sometimes we see dogs whose tails curl over and lay on the back. Some judges penalize this too gay tail. However, it is preferable to the undesirable low set tail.

Naturally bobbed tails are found in some lines of Toy Fox Terriers. These shortened tails can present problems for the show breeder. Some natural bobs, as they are called, are born with no tail at all. Natural bob litters often contain pups with tails of varying lengths. Rarely are natural bobs born with tails of the desirable length. This can make docking difficult for the person dreaming of future champions. Clearly, if the breeder subtracts the full three-fifths called for in the UKC standard, they'll have a tail that is too short for the show ring. Likewise, docking to the 3rd or 4th joint may be irrelevant with a short natural bob.

Some breeders, particularly those who don't like tail docking, value and include the natural bobs in their breeding programs. Due to the difficulty in assessing correct length, many other breeders prefer to exclude natural bobs from their kennels. In years past, the "NB," or natural bob designation, was included after the dog's registered name on UKC pedigrees. Since 1982, however, the NB designation no longer appears after the dog's color on the registration papers. Therefore, it does not appear on current pedigrees. This can make tracing the prevalence of natural bobs difficult, although it will still appear beside the names of dogs registered prior to November 1982.

Coat

The TFT's short, satiny coat is one of the breed's most distinctive features. A Toy Fox Terrier's physical condition is generally reflected by the condition of his coat. Parasites, both internal and external, can cause the coat to become rough, dry and dull. The coat of a TFT, in good condition, appears shiny and is soft to the touch. The skin should be firm, but pliable. The hair is short and rather fine in texture. It should never be coarse, long or wiry. The hair should be thick enough to cover the body well. The coat, however, is finer and sparser on the insides of the legs and on the belly. The coat can be slightly longer on the back of the neck and shoulders. One of the pleasures of the TFT coat is its ease of maintenance. With an occasional bath and a light brushing your TFT will always look his best.

Body Color and Markings

Many people are struck by the flashy coloring of the Toy Fox Terrier. Proper color and markings are easily seen at a glance in the show ring. Indeed, novices often place undue emphasis on the portion of the standard relating to color and markings. While proper color and markings are undeniably important, breeders must beware of placing so much emphasis on markings that they forget about the total dog. It is certainly true, however, that correct markings can do much to add to the beauty of a good TFT.

UKC and AKC standards allow for three acceptable color combinations: white, black and tan, white/black, and white/tan (to most accurately describe color, TFT breeders should always place the predominate color first when describing their dogs). In addition, the AKC standard allows white, chocolate and tan. The chocolate color has long been a disqualification in UKC since it was considered a color inherited from Chihuahuas. Maltese or blue coloration is a disqualification in both AKC and UKC. Any solid color or any other colored markings are considered serious faults.

The tan in the white and tan may be of varying shades. Seldom do we see a tan as deep as the tan on the cheeks and muzzle of a tri-colored TFT. Shades may vary from a red cast to a light, almost lemony hue. Some tan areas may be shaded with interspersed black hairs. If the overall look appears more black than tan, the entry should be penalized. Other tans will have the black hair on the muzzle, which creates a mask.

Primarily white body color has been a hallmark of the Fox Terrier since the late 1700's. For this reason, primarily white color became an early requirement in the TFT standard. The white on the Toy Fox Terrier should be a pure, clean white, much like the color of freshly fallen snow. The white must not have a cream, biscuit or ivory tinge. The dog's body must be more than one-half white. Any deviation from this is disqualified in the show ring. Determining whether white predominates on the body should include an examination of the color under the chest, or brisket, and the tuck up. Please note: Leg color is not included as part of the body when determining the degree of white present.

Solid black, chocolate, or tan located below the wrist on the front legs or below the hock joints on

Ch. "PR" Kadelon's Carmelle, owned by Bernice McDermitt, of Wapakoneta, Ohio, is an excellent white and tan TFT.

This young TFT is primarily white, but her black coloration extends down her front leg. Such markings are faulted in the show ring.

the rear legs should be faulted. The AKC standard penalizes solid colors below the elbow on the front legs. In a TFT with a black spot on the hip or the rump, in which the color extends under the tail, a tiny spot of tan is sometimes noted on the rectum. This should not be penalized unless there is an excessive amount of tan color. Likewise, shoulder spots sometimes extend down the upper portion of the leg above the elbow. Very often there will appear a coin-sized spot of tan on the upper leg. Such a tiny spot may also appear when a black marking overlaps the bottom of the rib cage. Tan shading or very small tan spots are undesirable, but should not be faulted. Generally these are only occasional occurrences.

The standards permit some ticking. Ticking, or speckling, is a small area of colored hair found on the white background. Undoubtedly, ticking is an influence that hales from the Smooth Fox Terrier. Through selective breeding, ticking has been minimized, but you can still find TFTs with some speckling. While ticking is not desirable, dogs with otherwise good markings should not be heavily penalized for its presence. TFTs with ticking often have lots of shiny black coloring and rich tan trim. The introduction of such TFTs into a breeding program might provide the pigment needed to add deep coloring into the line.

While markings on the head may be difficult to assess for the breeder whelping his first Toy Fox Terrier litter, body markings are easier to determine. The spots of color on the body will grow and expand as the pup develops. The tan, which may line a black spot or markings running down the leg, may be barely visible or appear minimal in the newborn. However, by the time the puppy is two to three months old, they will become evident.

Both registries have a number of color disqualifications. Both require that white be predominate on the body, that the head be *less* than half white, that head and ear color be the same color as body spots, and that only the color combinations

This puppy has several color faults. His body coloring is predominantly black, not white. Note that the color extends below his hock. In addition, this heavily boned pup is overly large for his age.

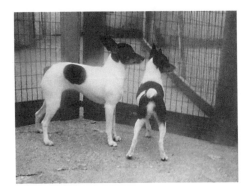

A dog with a very poor topline. Note the roached back and excessive tuck-up. In addition, this natural ~~Best of Breed~~ dog has no tail.

listed in the standard be allowed. AKC additionally disqualifies blazes that touch the eye.

Frankly, I think color is the least of our problems in this breed and I hate to see an otherwise excellent representative of the breed lose to an inferior specimen based upon a minor color fault. Do we really believe that color that descends a half-inch beyond the elbow is going to be replicated in that dog's progeny? Although the body is to be over 50% white, how closely are we to cull those who are 50/50? It is my opinion that a breeder needs to occasionally add more pigment to his lines by breeding to some of those with lots of shiny black and deep rich tan. My experience has been that generations of mostly or all white bodies will lead to adults that gray too early. I do not discriminate against fading or graying in the older TFT in the ring. I think it is important that we see how adult dogs hold up over time. Additionally, I don't understand how we can decry ticking when it is so terrier and the Fox Terrier often has it to a great degree.

A typey chocolate Jamoca Chip owned by Margi Hill and Karen Strauss.

Movement

Some owners are apt to place little importance on the movement of the Toy Fox Terriers. After all, this is a toy breed, they say, not a hunting dog that spends all day in the field. Anyone who's lived with a TFT, however, can attest to the fact that he is a vital, active dog. Indeed, as he runs around the house jumping from chair to chair and from lap to lap, he may receive more exercise than many larger breeds. The TFT is a long-lived breed. With proper conformation and movement, he will remain hardy and vigorous throughout his life.

It is often said that movement is the truest indicator of good conformation. There is something to be said for this, as gaiting is a good measure of overall sound-ness. Proper gait just isn't possible without proper conformation and structure. Many faults that may not be apparent when the dog is posed come quickly to light when the dog is moved. If you went to purchase a used car, you would not be con-tent to merely look at it, no matter how close your examination. You'd insist on tak-ing the car for a test drive, because you'd be more likely to feel or hear some defect. Likewise, when the dog moves, you may well see some fault that had previously escaped your notice.

In the show ring, the gait is examined from three angles. The judge will look at the dog from the side, in profile, as he gaits around the ring. He will also look at the dog from the rear, as he moves away from him, and from the front while the dog approaches. This gives the judge a balanced view of the dog from every angle and allows him to best assess the TFT's movement. The dog will be expected to trot, which is the canine's most efficient and natural gait. When a dog walks, three feet are always in contact with the ground. When the dog trots, only two feet touch the ground. The trot is called two-beat lateral gait, in which opposing diagonals move together. In other words, the right front foot moves at the same time as the left rear foot, and the left front and right rear foot move together. Good physical structure is very important when a dog trots, for in this mode he must rely on speed and balance.

Profile Movement

The gait, as seen in profile, is the most difficult for the novice to properly assess. That's because so many interrelated parts of the body can be seen at the same time. The judge will be looking for a free and easy gait. He'll check the topline to make sure that it stays level when the dog moves. A dog whose back bobs up and down is not an efficient mover. He's wasting his effort with up and down, rather than forward, motion.

Balanced angulation is essential to good movement when viewed in profile. A Toy Fox Terrier whose front and rear angulation is equal will have the proper rhyth-mic gait. Though a TFT may have poor angulation (too straight in the shoulders and stifles) his gait will still appear more balanced than the dog with mismatched angulation. His gait, however, will not be as efficient and free as the properly angulated dog. The length of his stride will be correspondingly shorter and he'll have to take more steps to cover the same distance. He will lack that beautiful, smooth stride, with good reach and drive that's so desirable.

Let's think for a moment about the way an automobile operates. Generally, the rear wheels of your car provide the propulsive power that drives the car forward. The front wheels set the course of direction. If your front wheel should sink into a mud hole, the propulsive power from the rear will probably be sufficient to dislodge the vehicle. If the rear wheel should go down, however, it'll be much more difficult to free the car. If you should suffer a sudden blowout when you're on the highway, you'll have an easier time controlling the car if one of the rear tires goes flat than if a front tire is affected. Since the front wheels are instrumental in controlling direction (steering), a blowout of a front tire, particularly at high speed, creates a dangerous situation. A blowout on the rear may temporarily affect control, but you will likely be able to safely maneuver your car to the side of the road.

Now, let's consider the dog's body as an efficient car-like machine. His little legs act much like the wheels of a car. The dog generates his power from the rear. Without strong muscular thighs and sufficient angulation, he won't be able to develop the power necessary to effortlessly propel him forward. His front legs, just like the car's front wheels, are responsible for changes in direction. They must have the angulation to enable the dog to make rapid turns and changes of direction. When the dog is ready to stop, the front legs and shoulders must be powerful enough to absorb the initial impact. With proper flexibility and balance, the dog can pull up abruptly and appear to stop on a dime.

The judge hopes to see free and effortless movement. He'll be paying attention to the dog's length of stride. He wants to see the rear legs reach well under the dog, then straighten out, driving the dog forward and following through vigorously. This long stride will provide the maximum in power. He'll want to see the front legs reach smoothly forward from the shoulder, without breaking the straight line from shoulder to foot. The foot must then hit the ground smoothly, drive backward and follow through, although the front follow through should not extend as far as the rear. It's important that the front legs be able to keep up with those driving rear legs. If the front stride does not match that of the rear, it causes interference and the dog may sidewind or swing the rear. This, of course, makes for an inefficient gait and impedes forward movement.

The feet must clear the ground cleanly. The dog should never appear to be tripping over his feet. However, they should just clear the ground. Neither the front or rear feet should be raised abruptly upward. A dog that raises his feet is wasting energy, which should always be directed forward, rather than upward. A dog that flings or kicks his feet upward while gaiting breaks the clean forward motion we want to see. This inefficient motion tires the dog unnecessarily. That being said, the degree of the lifting of the front legs needs to be considered. The hackney gait is a fault in which the canine lifts the front feet to an exaggerated degree, resembling the gait of the Miniature Pinscher or Italian Greyhound. Many TFTs lift the front feet, but not nearly to this degree and should not be faulted. The judge will have to make a decision as to whether this lift of the front legs constitutes a hackney gait by comparing the TFT gait to the gait of the Miniature Pinscher or the Italian Greyhound.

Rear Movement

The judge will want to examine your dog's movement from the rear to ascertain if his hindquarters move properly. As the dog begins to move, he'll be in a slow trot. At this slower speed, his rear feet should move straight forward. In a dog with a good rear, the rear pasterns will be exactly vertical and moderately apart. If the dog moves with his pasterns too wide, he'll have a waddling, duck-like action. If the pasterns are too close, particularly if they brush together, they will interfere with the necessary free and easy movement. Either fault robs the dog of power. The hocks should not turn inward, which indicates cowhocks. Sometimes a dog that is minimally cowhocked, will have escaped the judge's attention on individual examination. However, as the dog moves, the judge will be able to see that telltale convergence of the hocks. Similarly, the hocks should not turn outward. While this type of action is rarely seen, it should nonetheless be penalized.

As the dog picks up speed and moves into a fast trot, the placement of the feet will change somewhat. As speed increases, the dog has to adjust his footfall to maintain balance. Therefore, he inclines his feet inward so that they converge on a center line under his body. This convergence is dubbed "single tracking" because the dog's front and rear feet will hit a single centered line. This phenomenon can best be seen on a sandy, damp beach where the dog's pads will leave an imprint. It's also possible to observe this on snow of the proper texture. The next time the opportunity presents itself, try trotting your dog on one of these surfaces. You'll be able to clearly see this centerline, single tracking movement as the dog trots.

As has been said, in the fast trot the legs will incline inward. There should be no deviation, however, in that straight unbroken line from the hips to the feet. The feet should still reach straight forward, hocks straight, with no side to side motion. In the good moving dog, with proper angulation, the judge will be able to see the pads of the rear feet on the follow through. This shows the judge that the dog moves powerfully, gets his feet well under him and follows through fully. It's a visible testament to the dog's rear drive.

Front Movement

The judge will also want to see the dog's movement from the front. As was previously discussed (see Forequarters) this is the most complicated and interrelated part of the dog's structure. In the very slow trot, the dog's legs should drop straight from the elbows to the feet and be parallel to each other. Just as in rear action, as the dog's speed increases, his front legs will converge on that imaginary center line.

Front movement is dependent on numerous factors in addition to correct shoulder layback. The construction of the rib cage is vitally important. The judge will look for interference in the elbow action. If the dog has a barrel chest, he'll have to swing his elbows wide to avoid the chest. This serious fault will be immediately apparent. The judge will also be looking for any unusual looseness in the front movement. He'll quickly detect any crossing over or weaving of the front legs, which would point to a loosely constructed shoulder. Paddling, where the front legs move in a canoe paddle motion, is the result of tied-in or inelastic shoulders. The judge will be looking at the feet and pasterns to be sure they reach straight forward. The front feet should neither turn inward or outward, nor should they be elevated so much as to approximate the Min Pin's hackney gait.

A properly moving Toy Fox Terrier is truly beautiful. With his head and tail held high, he steps out cleanly and crisply in a straightforward efficient manner. All of his body parts join to give him a harmonious, synchronized action. Once we understand the complexities of movement, it is truly amazing to see everything come together to produce that wonderful effortless gait. Good movement in a Toy Fox Terrier should be treasured and cherished, for it is a sure indication of a balanced well made dog.

Size

Size has long been a hotly debated topic in TFT circles. As we discussed in the history chapter, the pioneers in our breed were constantly confronted with disagreements as to proper TFT size. It was only through their never ending vigilance that the Toy Fox Terrier remained a true toy dog. As Dr. Fuhrman, long time owner of the United Kennel Club, reminded breeders, it takes only a short time to increase size. To keep the TFT a toy breed, however, requires continued work on the part of breeders.

The policies of the United Kennel Club have done much to firmly establish the proper size for the Toy Fox Terrier. Before entering any UKC licensed show, each Toy Fox Terrier is weighed. The standard states that all Toy Fox Terriers six months of age or older must weigh from three-and-one-half up to and including seven pounds. Puppies under six months may be shown in special non-licensed classes and may be under three-and-one-half pounds, but no dog of any age may be shown if it weighs over seven pounds. Thus, weight of developing puppies and adults have become a focus for UKC breeders.

There is no doubt that weight can fluctuate from show to show and two dogs of the same size might differ in weight as much as pound. Since scales used by show-giving clubs were of questionable accuracy—some weighing light and others heavy—one breeder took to carrying a set of standard weights to check the scales in case his dogs were weighed out of acceptable range. Some exhibitors were legendary in their ability to stack their TFT on a scale to get the desired weight—a gentle lift of the head worth a 1/2 pound or so. Of particular concern were those exhibitors who might severely restrict a TFT's rations just to make weight, often feeding the hungry dog immediately after weighing. Likewise, the owner of a tiny exhibit might feed his TFT before weighing to insure that it went over the lower limit. There were breeders who liked TFTs that weighed eight to ten pounds who were excluded from competition. At one time these breeders petitioned, to no avail, that their larger TFTs be allowed to be shown as a variety.

Perhaps because of doubts about weight as a determinant of size, the AKC standard utilizes height. This standard dictates that the TFT must be 8 1/2 inches up to 11 1/2 inches at the withers. This term refers to the highest point of the shoulders at the point where neck and back meet. The standard states that a nine to eleven inch range is preferred.

Each dog is not measured before AKC competition the way they are weighed before UKC conformation shows. Instead, measuring is at the discretion of the judge, who may call for an official wicket to accurately measure the dog. Exhibitors in the ring have the right to ask the judge to measure any dog in the ring, as long as this is requested prior to every dog in the ring being individually gaited and examined.

The wicket is a bar supported by two expandable legs. The bar is set prior to measurement and checked with a tape measure. The exhibitor of the dog being measured is asked to observe and confirm the measurement of the wicket legs. The TFT is stacked on the table while the wicket is placed from the rear at the withers. If the question is one of being too large, the legs of the wicket will lift off the

This tiny, 3 pound female has the classic domed, or apple, head. The roundness of her foreskull shows clearly in this photo. Otherwise, her conformation is very nice.

A TFT that just kept growing. This dog matured at 21 pounds! This may be a "throwback" to the TFT's Fox Terrier ancestry.

table if the TFT is over 11 1/2 inches. More obvious will be a TFT not achieving 8 1/2 inches by not meeting the bar at the withers.

Variations in TFT Size

Both AKC and UKC standards allow for a lot of variability in size. Whether 3 1/2 pounds or 8 1/2 inches, the lower end of the size spectrum is dwarfed by the larger 7-pound or 11 1/2 inch specimen. Such variability allows for breeder preferences for size and it does not eliminate dogs that may excel in valuable breed characteristics. This wide variation in size, however, can make it difficult for the breeder to predict the size of dogs he can expect in any given litter. Breeding for consistent size is one of the most challenging aspects facing the Toy Fox Terrier breeder.

SELECTING A TFT

Buying your first Toy Fox Terrier is exciting. You've probably met a TFT owned by someone else and can't wait to have one of your own. It's better to slow down, however, and give some hard thought to your purchase. The worst thing you can do is to impulse-buy any puppy. Don't give in to the desire to call breeders across the county until you locate a puppy that will be air shipped to you in 48 hours! After all, the Toy Fox Terrier is a long-lived breed and this dog will be with you for many years. It's best not to dash out and buy the first cute puppy you see. The more that you learn about the breed, the better your chance of finding a dog that will suit your needs and provide you with years of companionship and joy.

When you find the breeder with the type of TFT you like, you may still have to wait for a breeding to take place and/or for puppies to be born. However, even this wait will not guarantee that you may lay claim to a puppy. Most responsible breeders are breeding to a standard of perfection and litters are planned to improve the breed. The breeder for show and/or breeding will retain some puppies. This, coupled with low litter numbers (2-3 puppies in an average litter) means that TFT puppies are generally in high demand. TFT breeders will keep the puppies they need to continue their breeding program and to show, and will be very choosy in placing any remaining puppies at pets.

Breeders will want to get to know you personally. They will want to know who will be the care giver for the puppy; what are the ages of any children in the home; whether or not there is a fenced yard; where will the puppy live (TFTs are not dogs that can be kept outside); will the puppy be spayed at the appropriate time, etc. You may be asked to sign a contract guaranteeing certain conditions will be met.

Selecting a puppy should be a thoughtful process. It involves goal setting at the start, then lots of research. Be thorough and you may be rest assured when your puppy is ready to come to your home that you have a puppy that fits your family, and comes from a breeder with whom you will have a long-time relationship.

WHAT DO YOU WANT?

What part will the dog play in your life? Are you looking for a pet that will be a wonderful companion? Many TFTs come to be regarded as one of the family. Many families have always had TFTs and would accept no other breed. Do you have children in your home? Perhaps you are buying a Toy Fox Terrier that will serve primarily as your children's companion. Have you always dreamed of having a show dog? Dog showing is a wonderful family hobby. Will you want to breed your dog? If so, size and quality will be a consideration. You won't want to buy a dog with a serious fault if you plan on eventually breeding. All of these things will have to be taken into consideration.

A responsible breeder can be a great help to you in locating just the right dog. In order for him to do this, however, you'll have to be honest with him. Tell the breeder what you want. Remember, the breeder has invested time, effort and money in his dogs. His concern for them extends far beyond the money he will receive. No breeder wants to hear complaints and no buyer wants to be disappointed with his purchase. With cooperation, both of you can be satisfied. You'll have the dog that suits you and fulfills your needs, and the breeder will know that his dog has found a loving home.

WHERE TO BUY

All TFT puppies are cute. But where and from whom you buy is very important. Stay out of pet shops lest you rescue a potentially defective puppy when you are vulnerable to urges to have a puppy now. Pet-shop buying reinforces the practice of running puppy mills. Buy directly from a reputable breeder. Where can you locate such a breeder? Access the web sites of the American Toy Fox Terrier Club (www.atftc.com) and the National Toy Fox Terrier Association (www.ntfta.net-firms.com) to find a list of breeders in your state or nearby states. The American Kennel Club (AKC) web site (www.AKC.org) and the United Kennel Club (UKC) site (www.ukcdogs.com) may also be helpful. Both may be used to find conformation shows you may wish to attend. I would recommend that you attend several to get a feel for the TFT you prefer and to note which breeders produce that style. After the competition, you may wish to ask questions of the breeder if he/she is present or obtain information on how to contact the breeder. By doing so you can learn of any current or upcoming litters and arrange to see their facility and breeding stock. There are also dog magazines on the newsstands that offer classified advertising for most breeds. Don't be disappointed or discouraged if you are put on a waiting list for puppies. As a matter of fact, be wary of the breeder who seems to have a constant supply of puppies. Some breeders cross the line into breeding irresponsibly for financial gain.

SELECTING THE RIGHT PUPPY

Of course, you want to select a healthy puppy. Even though you aren't a veterinarian, there are some indicators you can check. Look for an overall healthy appearance. The pup's eyes should be clear and bright, not runny. His coat should be shiny and free of any rough patches or bald spots. Lift up the lip and look at the gums. They should be bright pink. Avoid the puppy with white gums, as he may have a severe case of worms. Watch the puppies play and see if they appear frisky and alert. These are good overall indicators of health, but a thorough vet inspection will reveal any problems immediately. We ask new owners of our puppies to schedule a vet visit within a week of purchasing the puppy.

What size of puppy do you want? If this is a home with children, you might want to choose a larger, heavy-boned puppy. If the puppy is going to a home with adults only, the smaller puppy may be selected as a lap dog. By four weeks of age, the breeder should have a good idea how large each puppy may get.

What kind of personality do you want, remembering that most TFTs have boundless energy, particularly their first year? However, some puppies are more introverted or laid back and may be more suited for the mature buyer. Others are what I call "rocket dogs". They need lots of stimulation and exercise. Perhaps a physically active owner or a family with several older children may be able to wear this type of puppy out!

Asa and Sepia—Best Buddies. Photo by David C. Ring.

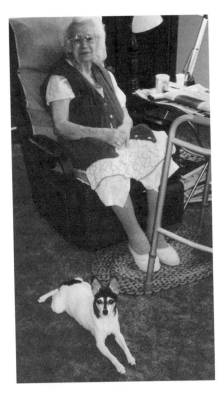

The Golden Years.

Even the rocket dogs, however, slow down between 1 and 2 years of age.

Do you prefer a male or female puppy? Please do not be blinded by the sexist notion that little girl dogs will be sweet and loving while little boy dogs will be rough and ready for action. Males can be just as loving a pet as a female and just as gentle. Conversely, we have experienced many rocket female dogs! A male puppy that is neutered early will likely not lift his leg for urination. Our current house pets include a neutered male and spayed female TFTs. The female loves to fetch and will bring back her toy again and again to be thrown. She is the first to alert and bark and is always wired for action. The male is in his element quietly chewing a rawhide chip while plastered to my side for protection. My point is the old labels and myths about which sex makes the best pet should be discarded. Today, female children who were once relegated to playing with dolls in their toy kitchens are finding opportunities to participate in formerly male sports and activities. We would do well to allow our TFTs to be recognized for the individuals they are, and not be bound by stereotypes based on gender.

THE OLDER DOG

Breeders occasionally will place a retired show or breeding TFT in a pet home for a nominal or no fee other than that required neutering. Such TFTs may or may not be house broken. The older dog is, however, past the destructive chewing stage. A young male champion of ours, larger than what we wanted for our breeding program, went to a family home with a school-aged child and a cat. Within two weeks I receive a picture of the TFT lying on the young man's lap, along with the cat, with a note saying the TFT, almost two years old, was completely housebroken. Another 8 year old champion female went to live with a college administrator. The two bonded

An active older dog: Dolly Peterson. Owned by Kim Peterson, New London, WI.

immediately and currently enjoy long walks and watching TV together. Future plans include enrolling this veteran TFT in agility classes for seniors! I asked the new owner, Kim, for her recommendations for adopting an older dog and she wrote: "Prepare your home the same way you would if you were bringing a puppy home. Even if it turns out that chewing or other destructive behavior isn't an issue, there's a certain peace of mind that comes with knowing the dog is in a 'safe' area. Have some sort of hideaway that the dog can call her own—a crate, dog bed with high sides, a pile of blankets in the corner, or the like. At a minimum, assume that you'll have to do a refresher course in house training. Ditto for basic obedience training, especially because TFTs (like so many breeds of small dogs) are often under-trained. Also assume that, having just been separated from one home/family, the dog will be overly sensitive to being left alone at first. As with a puppy, start by leaving it alone for a short period of time and gradually increase the time alone. For the first week or two, try to make sure that you or a family member will be home with the dog pretty much all day, to help her bond with you and to help her get acclimated to her new home. But even if you are on vacation, try to maintain some sort of a routine to help the dog settle in faster. Even simple things like always using the same door to let the dog out are important. If the dog isn't used to living in a house, expect to teach the unexpected such as how to go up and down stairs (start one from the top-bottom and gradually increase), a mirror is nothing to fear, the TV set does not have real people/animals inside, etc. Don't worry if the dog doesn't eat much during the first few days. Have a least some of the dog's 'usual' food and treats on hand when you bring her home. If you want to change foods, gradually mix in the new food over the span of a week or so. According to our vet, expect the transition to take a least two months." The American Toy Fox Terrier Association website has contacts for rescued TFTs. There is generally an adoption fee, which includes spaying/neutering. Some of the TFTs have been abandoned or abused, others may have behavioral problems, and others may have lost their owners through death or are unable to be shown or bred. Saving and rehabilitating a TFT can be most rewarding for the right person/family.

Stacy and Asa. Photo by David C. Ring.

TFTS AND CHILDREN

Dogs and children have a unique rapport. In fact, owning a pet can be a very special experience for a child. A dog can provide a youngster with unconditional love and a deep sense of friendship. Psychologists have recently discovered that dogs and children develop especially close bonds. By using dogs they have managed to reach many emotionally disturbed and withdrawn children. Dogs also aid in developing the growing child's character. By caring for and training the dog, children learn responsibility. The dog/child bond also helps to instill a sense of understanding, kindness and compassion.

Many Toy Fox Terriers prove to be fantastic children's companions. As a toy dog, however, the TFT is not suited to all children. When I am asked whether TFTs are good with children, I turn the question around and say, "are the children good with TFTs?" While the TFT is a hardy little dog, as a puppy he is prone to breaking legs and cannot tolerate rough handling or jumping off of furniture. The decision to purchase a TFT for your child must be based on your assessment of the child's personality and behavior. A sedate child will learn to handle even the smallest TFT with tenderness. A more active youngster may find the perfect companion in a larger TFT. For the heavy-handed toddler, who's likely to hit or pull ears, I would recommend that parents wait until the child can understand how to interact with a TFT. I had TFTs before I had children. I had to teach my children how to relate to the TFTs. It can be done, but it demands patience, firmness, and supervision.

No matter what size TFT is best for your child, there are some factors that must be borne in mind. No matter how desperately the child wants a Toy Fox Terrier, parents must remember that dog ownership is a family venture. As a parent, you have ultimate responsibility for the dog. You must teach the child how to care for and handle the dog properly. If the child forgets to feed the dog, then you must step in. You must be prepared to care for the dog without resentment. If you don't want the dog every bit as much as your child does, then don't make the purchase.

PURCHASING A PET

While most breeders hope to have a whole litter of show quality puppies, this rarely happens. It's far more likely that there will be pups in each litter who lack some fine point required for success in the show ring. Such fine points will probably escape you and certainly not be noticed by the general public. While the puppy many not have what it takes to be a show winner, he still comes from the same stock as his more illustrious brethren. He's been reared in the same way and received an identical amount of love and care.

Just because your puppy is labeled as pet quality does not mean that he's inferior. Indeed, the difference between a show and pet quality puppy may not be outwardly discernible. Perhaps the puppy does meet the standard of a show dog but does not have the potential size or characteristics deemed most important by the breeder. This does not impair the dog's ability to function as a wonderful companion. In other cases, the breeder may retain only one or two TFTs to show, and place the other perfectly lovely puppies in loving pet homes. Please realize that the pet quality dog is every bit as intelligent and loving as his show quality littermates.

In purchasing a pet, temperament will be of prime importance. By closely observing a litter, you'll see indications of future temperament. Spend some time watching the litter at play. See how they interact with people, including their breeder. Chances are you'll be able to spot the most aggressive pup, the quiet one and the one who's most attentive. You want a sensible puppy with a stable personality. Pet owners often say that their puppy chose them. That's not a bad way to make a selection!

Take me! Litter owned by Marsha Shively, Ft. Wayne, IN.

SHOW AND BREEDING STOCK

A show quality puppy is one who conforms to the standard and can be expected to win in the show ring. It can be tricky to pick future show winners. Beware of breeders who sell puppies labeled as show quality at 8 weeks of age. It is extremely difficult at a young age to know whether a puppy will mature as a show winner. One of my favorite dogs was Ch. Meadowoods Got A Notion. I had a notion he would be a show ring winner at 8 weeks. But would you pay several hundred dollars for someone's notion about a puppy's future potential? The only guaranteed way to be assured of getting a show quality dog is to purchase an older dog that's already out there consistently winning. Short of that, realize that the show puppy will likely be 3-6 months old and not the baby puppy that is so adorable. Still, if you have your heart on a puppy, there are some points to bear in mind. Familiarize yourself with the standard, learn what you like and choose a breeder whose stock appeals to you. A breeder who's been working with his bloodline for years, and knows how his stock matures, will have a good idea which puppies will grow into superior TFTs. He will have the advantage of knowing how the puppy's ancestors matured and what they looked like at a young age. Expect the breeder to carefully evaluate your stewardship of his best puppy. Remember, breeders work many years to produce the best possible specimen. They are allowing you to exhibit the result of years of study and effort. Don't be offended if you feel you are proving yourself to be worthy. Some breeders may insist on co-ownership so that they can be involved in the decision-making as to the TFT's exhibition and breeding schedule.

Expect to pay more for the show quality puppy. You may also find that the show quality pup is slightly older. The breeder may well have recognized his potential and held him until a show home could be found. Since the breeder has more invested in the puppy, he'll ask a higher price.

In choosing the show quality puppy, there are certain things you'll want to see. It's obvious that the dog should not have any points listed as faults in the standard. A good head, sound legs, a strong topline, high tailset and good movement are musts. If you plan on breeding, choose a medium-sized dog. In addition, look for that extra something. A dog, which exudes that indefinable class, will generally go far. If you are looking at a group of show quality puppies and there's one you just can't take your eyes off of, pick him. If you are new to the breed, you will no doubt have to depend a great deal on the word of the breeder as to the quality of the prospect. In the end your success will depend on the trust you placed in this breeder.

There are additional points you should keep in mind. You want your Toy Fox Terrier to be capable of producing healthy, strong puppies of good quality. Look for

The boys. Owned by David Ring and Jody Guillot. Photo by David Ring.

An adorable seven week old puppy bred by Deborah J. Hays. Photo by Cindy K. Rogers.

First Bath for Spike. Owned by Jay and Leslie Miller.

Oliver, owned by John and Judy Lengyel, loves to swim in the cool Minnesota lake beside his vacation home.

This is a test! How many TFTs can you spot? Photo by Marsha Shively.

Debbie Fair: Human mattress.

National Grand Champion Pegasus Jacobs Mighty Mickey owned by Dianna James.

Lalique Jumpin' Jack Flash bred by Dorothy Fisher and owned by Lynn Heiden.

Twas the night before Christmas. Marsha Shivelely's TFT sneak a peek.

White and chocolate champion owned by Dana Plonkey.

Thais loves to lure course. Owned by David Ring and Judy Guillot.

Eat and sleep—That's all they do at this age! Photo by Judy Threlfall.

The first TFT in the Toy Group at Madison Square Garden: Dana and "Butchie," Ch. Valcopy Butch Cassidy.

Want to be licked to death? Photo by Judy Threlfall.

Fashionable lounge-wear modeled by these lovelies owned by Chip and Debbie Fair.

That's not a bunny—it's Tuffy, owned by the VanAllens.

A beautiful head shot of Gracie, owned by Mark and Judy Threlfall. AKC CH UKC GRCH Chestnut's Miss Congeniality, bred and exhibited by Judy Chestnut Threlfall.

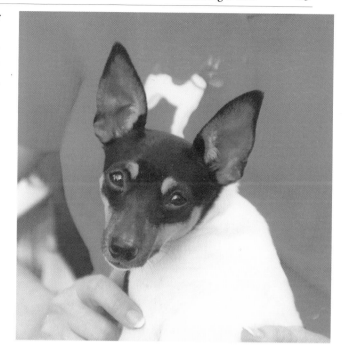

Lani, the TFT, with best friends Kalima and Keoki. Photo by John David Zieba.

Ch. Valcopy Kasey Kahne.

National Grand Champion Kadelon's Taffy Apple owned by Diane McDermitt. The first tan and white TFT to achieve National Grand title in 1988.

Ch. Valcopy Way Cool Thriller.

Tude, owned by Ramona Bajorek, bursts out of the tunnel. Photo by Ken Gee.

the dog that comes from a long line of healthy dogs. Females should descend from a line of bitches that whelp easily and freely. Ask about the percentage of oversize or undersize dogs produced from that bloodline. There will be some, but if the majority of dogs conform to the size you like, the bitch will be apt to produce that size. Finally, look for the names of males and females, in the pedigree, who have a reputation for producing top quality offspring. If your TFT comes from a long line of males and females that produced champions, he's most likely to continue the tradition.

PAPERS AND REGISTRATION

The breeder may present you with UKC and/or AKC registration papers for you to register the puppy in your own name. If so, please send them in immediately so you do not forget or misplace these papers in the excitement of bringing a puppy home. When selling puppies as pets, many breeders stipulate in writing that the papers will be sent when proof of neutering or spaying is provided, as pet puppies are not to be bred. The AKC allows breeders to limit the pet puppy to performance events like Obedience or Agility and disallow registration of offspring of this pet puppy. It may appear that the breeder is assuming too much control, but in reality, the breeder is being responsible by supporting the breed standard.

CARING FOR YOUR TFT

 It's a momentous day. Your puppy comes home. Hopefully you will have already purchased the food that the puppy is currently eating. If it is not a premium puppy food, gradually switch to a brand high in protein and calcium. Feeding the best for the first year will pay off in the long run. Dog treats that were being fed will also need to be on your shopping list. You may wish to bring along a container to bring home water that the puppy is used to drinking. We recommend that you eventually mix it with your water to complete the transfer. We believe this is especially important if well water is involved at either end of the transfer process.

Although your TFT will likely look upon you as his personal toy, it would be wise to have dog toys on hand. TFTs love a large, LIGHT toy. Somehow it makes them feel like superman to get their teeth into a toy almost as large as them and parade around the room. We also use the little Beanies that McDonalds gave away years ago, if they do not have dangerous hardware, easily lost eyes, etc. We find them on EBAY or at sales. They are just the right size for an 8-week-old puppy. We've found that a large stuffed toy also gives your puppy something to snuggle with in bed when he misses his littermates.

I hope you will have bought a size #100 Vari-Kennel pet carrier or a similar type crate in which to bring him home. We prefer this type crate, as it is more "den-like" than wire crates, easily cleaned, and protects the TFT within from drafts and intrusions from strangers- canine or otherwise. We are absolute believers that every dog should have his own portable home. Dogs are safely contained while traveling and this carrier can be his room/den in your home. Our dogs travel hundreds of miles annually in our van, sleeping blissfully on their fleece rugs in their crates. Motels are comforted by the fact that our TFTs are crated while staying overnight. Try to register while your dogs bounces around in the car and you may be turned away.

Decide in what room or rooms the puppy will be contained until housebroken. We use our kitchen and dining area, because of the vinyl flooring which is easily

That's a mouthful! Photo by Dianna James.

cleaned. We have to puppy proof the room by removing items that we do not wish chewed or broken. This destructive phase can go on for 6 months and we have some that continued till a year of age. Your planning should be the same as if a crawling infant was to visit. Eliminate electrical cords, all breakables, and anything that could be harmful if ingested (plants, under counter chemicals, etc.). At the outset your hands are going to be full just house training this puppy, let alone trying to teach not to chew books or electrical cords. House training is often frustrating, so do yourself a favor and eliminate other problems before they happen.

Purchase baby/pet gates that will prevent the puppy from slipping into other rooms. Note that your TFT puppy may be able to slip through the openings in many gates. We have backed up such gates with cheap plastic totes to keep the puppy in until he is too big to fit through the gate. We do not allow puppies access to our carpeted rooms. Carpeting is difficult to clean once soiled and unless deodorized that spot will be used again and again.

We organize the room by setting up an exercise pen (ex pen). The new plastic ones are light, easy to clean, don't mar floors, and make climbing out difficult. Most are made up of eight panels, but we use only four in the beginning. On the floor, we lay down a plastic tarp and put newspapers down on top of the tarp. We attach the puppy's food and water dishes to the ex pen and put his crate in the pen with the door removed. Now he has access to his bed, food and water and can use the papers if you are unable to get him outside in time. This also eliminates the need to get up in the middle of the night to take the puppy out. By approximately five to six months of age, you can attach the kennel door and close it at night, then immediately take the puppy out when you get up. However, this will be successful only as long as the puppy is given the opportunity to eliminate right before being crated and is not confined for more than 5-6 hours. After one year, the puppy will probably be able to be crated for up to 8 hours, provided he has been given a chance to eliminate before being placed in the crate. If you are working and away from home, this is a humane setup for your puppy. Please do not think that you can crate an 8-week-old puppy during your time away and expect anything but a messy crate when you return. It is true that they detest eliminating in their beds, but they also have limited ability to control their bladder or bowels for such a long time. Make the most of your at home time with your puppy and concede that he will have to use papers when you are not there. We have had some puppy owners use the indoor system that is very much like a doggy litter box. They have told us that their pups learned this system very quickly.

Housebreaking is all about catching your puppy being good and rewarding him. Scaring the puppy or hitting the puppy after an accident will only serve to make the puppy afraid of you, as he'll have no idea why you are terrorizing him. When you are with your puppy, I would recommend that you take him outside every half-hour. Have a treat in hand ready to reward him swiftly. TFTs are highly intelligent and will make the connection quickly. They will figure out easily that by going to the door you will let him out and he can earn his treat. We have found that a small piece of American cheese works very well for a training treat. I have found that there is a direct correlation between the trainer's diligence and the quickness of training. Get tied up on the phone or involved in a TV program and your sock will likely find a warm puddle or worse. Remember, don't be mad at the puppy, just vow to be more diligent in the future!

When you are home with your puppy, watch for him to exit his crate from sleep and take him outside. Reward him with a treat immediately after he potties and praise lavishly. Before urination puppies will start sniffing the floor for just the right spot. A protruding anus can denote defecation. In both cases get them outside quickly. After returning from a successful trip outside would be a good time to sit down on the floor and play with your pup. We practice a 6-inch rule with

Your TFT should be prohibited from jumping on and off furniture during puppyhood. Here is "PR" Five Oaks Brother John, owned by Chet and Kathleen Cornwell, of Aripeka, Florida, with his leg in a cast.

puppies. No puppy is to be higher than 6 inches off the floor- not on the bed, sofa, or even in your arms at the table. One sudden jump and a broken leg may result. We also require that everyone stay in place and not move around the room when a puppy is out for the same reason. Puppies play hard and vigorously, but they wear out just as quickly. Like a new baby they need to rest. Put them back in their pen after about 30 minutes of play and they will fall asleep in moments.

Puppies are not always available in spring or summer. Although we don't recommend taking a puppy home over the Christmas holidays (too many people; too many distractions), bringing a Christmas puppy home after New Year's day lightens the dark and cold of January and February by turning your focus on a puppy to nurture and enjoy. This is also a time when people spend more time at home. The problem with housebreaking in the Midwest or farther north is the outside temperature, which may likely be below zero, with or without huge snow accumulations. Even the hardest of hearts would have a problem pushing an 8-week-old puppy outdoors in such conditions. A compromise would be to set up an exercise pen in the attached garage and use it for the puppy. You may wish to ask the breeder for a newspaper that your puppy or his littermates piddled on. Put it in the ex pen to ignite in your puppy the impulse to relieve himself. A January puppy would also be a likely candidate for the indoor system already mentioned above.

As much as you may wish to hold your puppy on the way home, many do get car sick on this first trip, so bring extra newspapers for the crate. If you are traveling more than two hours, it may be necessary to let the puppy out to eliminate. Do not stop at a public rest stop, as they provide too much opportunity for disease and flea infestation. Isolate your puppy as much as possible during his infancy. If we see a nice grassy area adjacent to a restaurant, we will stop there and take turns eating. We carry disposable pick up bags, so that all waste is picked up and discarded. If you plan to walk your TFT, you will want to invest in a package of these pick-up bags, lest you irritate neighbors.

The breeder will supply you with information on shots and worming. If there is a health guarantee, this should be stipulated in writing. A time line for receiving registration papers should also be set down. If your puppy is to be your pet, the breeder may provide these papers after veterinary proof of neutering or spaying is provided. If the puppy is to be a show dog, you may expect to receive papers when you pick him up or soon after, if not yet back from the Registry.

One of the most important decisions you will make will be the decision about a veterinarian. You may already have an established relationship from owning a pet previously. If not, you may wish to contact other toy breed owners or breeders to ask whom their dog is seeing. Contact the local kennel club and ask for the names of some toy dog breeders in your vicinity. If you are lucky enough to live near your breeder, you might want to use his/her vet, since they will be familiar with the breed.

I have had clients drive 60 miles to use my vet, who has been treating TFTs for 30 years. While competence is fundamental, other factors enter into the decision. Are you comfortable with all of the vets in the practice? Do they have weekend hours? Is anyone on call for emergencies? Is there a mix of youth and experience in the practice? Does the vet show up-to-date expertise and empathy for you and your pet? Is the vet too harried to take sufficient time during an office call? Does the vet return phone calls in a timely manner? Do the office personnel make you feel welcome and are the veterinary technicians friendly and helpful? Only you can decide how important these answers might be. The selection of your vet should be a thoughtful one-not unlike the selection of your own personal physician.

Make an appointment to have your puppy veterinary-inspected within three days of his arrival home. This will assure that the puppy is indeed healthy. Any health concerns should be immediately relayed to the breeder. You will want to talk with the veterinarian about a vaccination schedule, fecal exam, flea, tick, and heart worm control, teeth cleaning, as well as the appropriate time for spaying or neutering.

As you can see, bringing home a new puppy is very similar to bringing home a baby, requiring forethought and planning, a large amount of attention during the first few months, but also full of excitement and rewards for mom or dad!

LONGEVITY

Toy Fox Terriers are animated, bouncy dogs with extraordinary energy packed into a compact frame. If we could bottle even a small percentage of the breed's abundant energy for resale, we'd all be rich. We are indeed fortunate that our breed is blessed with good health. While problems can occur in individual dogs, of course, there are no widespread health or genetic problems associated with the TFT. Since these little dogs become important family members, we are also fortunate that they are so long lived. I've heard of a Toy Fox Terrier that lived past twenty years of age. TFTs who live fifteen to eighteen years are not uncommon and one frequently hears of dogs who reach thirteen years of age. To insure that your Toy Fox Terrier lives a happy, healthy, full life, you, his owner, need to care for him sensibly. With proper care, you'll be able to enjoy the companionship of your TFT for many, many years.

SETTING THE RIGHT TONE

If your Toy Fox Terrier is to become a pleasurable companion, it's necessary to establish the right tone in your relationship from the very beginning. TFTs, particularly young puppies, are adorable. Beneath that cute exterior, however, can lie the heart of a tyrant. Even the smallest puppy can be amazingly willful. Owners of toy dogs are often apt to give in to their demanding youngster. After all, if he doesn't want to walk on a leash, why should he? It's so much easier to just scoop him up and tuck him under your arm. You may think it's amusing to watch your TFT puppy growl and attack someone's pant leg. When he's full-grown and the person he attacks is your elderly, frail grandmother, it's going to seem less charming. From the very beginning, strive for a well-mannered and well-trained dog. It's possible to be kind, generous and loving with your dog, without being indulgent and spoiling him unnecessarily.

To raise a well-mannered TFT it is best to decide that you will discipline your pup from the day you get him. Your TFT must know that you love him and you will be kind to him. However, he should also know that you are the boss and when you give an order it is not to be ignored. You'll be perfectly happy to lavish him with affection, but only when he pleases you and acts correctly. You will not tolerate a dog that is spoiled rotten. Be patient, be firm and be consistent. Your dog will soon come to understand what's expected of him.

It is important that you set boundaries early on for your puppy. The puppy must not be allowed to use those needle-sharp teeth on your skin or clothing. Remember again: What is cute at this period may not be so cute at adulthood. If a puppy decides your hand will be his chew toy, react with a loud startling sound. When the puppy's attention is diverted to an acceptable activity, praise him. You will have to decide whether you will allow the puppy to lick you, but it does help to reward licking with praise and biting with a scare. In this way the puppy can pursue what are normal mouthing activities in a way that reinforces that biting is never acceptable. Everyone in the family has to be on board or this training process will not work.

Similarly, no puppy should be allowed to growl during play or even at his feed dish. It is so easy for the biting behavior described above to emerge as a sequel to this growling as the puppy matures. Growling behaviors should be suppressed by startling sounds and with the puppy then rewarded with soothing praise when the growling stops. Some owners have found that shaking a soda can filled with rocks startles effectively when their own vocalization does not work. In some tough cases, you may need to imitate the pup's mother. A canine mother will discipline her whelps by picking them up by the scruff of the neck. In this situation a puppy will neither struggle nor bark. Therefore, if your pup persists in growling after being verbally startled, lift it by the scruff and scold it. I will lift the puppy and go eye to eye and give him a good talk. There can be no doubt in this relationship who is the dominant partner.

Hearing your puppy bark for the first time is the canine equivalent of your child's first word. But like the loquacious child who repeatedly asks questions, a barking TFT

A litter of seven week old puppies bred by Deborah J. Hays. Photo by Cindy K. Rodgers.

can aggravate you and your neighbors. Since some barking may be useful in protecting your household, the dog needs to know when enough is enough. Saying "quiet" in a strong, firm voice accompanied by a squirt of water in the face is an effective way to teach your puppy when barking is acceptable.

Please note that in all of these suggestions of how to discipline your puppy I am not advocating physical abuse. What you are trying to do is to extinguish the unsatisfactory behavior and reward the puppy for being good. A well mannered, obedient dog will only enhance your enjoyment of your pet.

WHERE WILL YOUR TFT SLEEP?

The grown TFT will generally select his own spot for sleeping. It may be a favorite chair, a warm spot by the fireplace or he may want to share your bed. For the puppy, however, you should provide a bed of some kind. This is best until your TFT is fully housebroken and can be trusted. There are a variety of dog beds on the market and they range from the simple to the elaborate. It's best to avoid wooden or wicker beds for the your puppy, however. Puppies have a tendency to chew on these materials while teething. Metal beds, with foam rubber mattresses, covered in a washable fabric are quite practical. I advocate for every TFT needing his own room in the form of a crate. Put a nice fleece-lined bed in the crate and some favorite toys (a puppy newly separated from his mother will take comfort from a large stuffed animal) and soon the puppy will view the crate as a desirable place. Giving the puppy a small piece of dog biscuit each time you put him in the crate will facilitate the process of the puppy associating his crate with comfort and safety.

This is my bed! Gr. Ch 'PR'
Hopkins Alibi bred by Eliza
Hopkins and owned by Deborah
J. Hays.

Given a chance, most
TFTs would prefer to share
your bed. After all, you consider it nice and comfy, and there's
nothing your dog likes better
than being close to you. If you
want your little dog to sleep on your bed, that is fine. It's important to remember,
however, that once you allow the dog to sleep with you, it will be very difficult to
reverse the practice. It's best to let your puppy grow up before you allow him to sleep
on the bed. Young puppies are particularly vulnerable. It is very easy to break those
little legs and a bad spill can even result in a broken neck. Jumping on and off beds,
or inadvertently falling from them, can present a very real danger. It is best to let your
puppy grow up and learn to judge heights before allowing him to share your bed. If
you do give in and allow the dog access to your bed, you may want to provide him
with a little footstool or other platform. Place the stool at the foot or side of the bed.
This way, your TFT will have an intermediate step to aid him in reaching the bed.

FEEDING YOUR TFT

Dog owners today are truly blessed to have at their fingertips an amazing array
of scientifically balanced dog foods. You may chose to feed your Toy Fox Terrier a
dry dog meal, a canned food or a semi-moist feed. No matter which kind of food
you select, you should examine the label to make sure that it is nutritionally complete. This will insure that your dog gets the proper blend of protein, fats, vitamins
and minerals.

Toy Fox Terriers thrive on a variety of diets. As a rule, dogs of this breed are
good eaters. Over the years, most breeders have experimented and determined the
diet that best suits their dogs. Ideas about the proper diet for a TFT vary. This simply illustrates that there is more than one way to feed a Toy Fox Terrier and still
maintain his condition. Unlike people, most dogs thrive on monotony. They are
creatures of habit. Once you find a food that is palatable to your dog, it is best to
stick with that food, rather than continuously switching brands. Encourage your

dog to develop good feeding habits. Ideally, he should eat his food within minutes of your setting it out for him. How much to feed daily is a challenge. It will change with the seasons, activity level and age of the dog. Just heed the signs of obesity and keep your dog slender (you should not be able to see ribs but you should easily feel them when you pick the dog up) and he will live a long active life.

Breeders are often asked how many times a day a Toy Fox Terrier should be fed. Growing puppies need twice as many calories as an adult dog. Depending on the puppy's age, he may require two to four feedings a day. It is best to check with the breeder, or your veterinarian, and follow their recommendations. We recommend free feeding of hard kibble for the first six months. Adult dogs need only one or two meals per day. I feed my dogs only once daily, but I do know that some breeders prefer to feed two smaller meals per day. Most dogs appreciate regularity. It is best to feed them at approximately the same time every day. This is one of the best ways to instill good eating habits.

Be sure to provide your dog with plenty of fresh, clean water. Ideally, he should have water available to him whenever he's awake. It's best to avoid allowing your dog to drink too much cold water after a hard play period. Give him a small drink, and when he's quieted down, offer more.

OBESITY AND THE TFT

Like many of the toy breeds, some TFT owners overindulge their pets. On average, one out of four dogs of any breed is overweight. In the toy breeds this figure may approximate one in two. This epidemic in canine obesity comes at the same time studies have revealed that obese pets expire as much as two years before their thinner counterparts. Obese dogs are more likely to experience diabetes, heart problems, and arthritis. As they age, obese dogs may experience hip dysplasia and back and joint pain. They

also pose a risk for surgery.

The UKC standard sets the weight of the TFT at six months, the time of beginning careers as show dogs, from 3 1/2 to 7 pounds. We routinely estimate the weight of a puppy at six months by counting on about one pound gain per month. To achieve this gain, most puppies are given unlimited feedings of nutritious puppy

Like adults, TFTs will overindulge.

foods. The problem enters at adulthood when the need for free feeding is over. It is a delicate balance to find the exact amount of food that will not cause your pet to gain weight, but still supply his nutritional and energy demands.

At adulthood, the scale may not always give you the information you need to make reasonable decisions about the weight of your TFT. In a toy breed there may be widespread variation in the weight of the dog, depending on how much the dog has eaten or how much exercise it may have received. Exhibitors who enter UKC shows will monitor their entry's weight carefully and adjust feedings accordingly as they near show time. I have seen TFTs over the weight limit, taken outside for exercise, and return 1/4 to 1/2 pound lighter and make weight for the show. Of course, there may be seven-pound TFTs who might look better at eight pounds and six pounders that might look better at five pounds. Simply put, the ideal weight for one dog may not be the ideal for another.

It is far better to examine each dog's physical condition and then determine how much food will maintain that ideal. The rib test can be revealing. One should be able to feel the ribs of a TFT without pressing, yet the ribs should not be seen rippling through the coat. Is there a definite tuck up behind the ribs on the underline? You should be able to start at the brisket (chest) and feel a dramatic rise when you get to the tuck up. The underline will likely be straight across on an overweight TFT. Finally, look down at your pet's body from above. The ideal body type is an hour glass shape. In other words, there should be a noticeable indentation behind the ribs, broadening again at the hips. The overweight TFT will not show this indentation and may appear sausage-like from above. If your TFT is found lacking on one of these tests, you may wish to address the problem before your pet becomes obese.

Fine tuning the amount each TFT can ingest can be a problem. If you have more than one TFT, the chances are great that each will get a different amount of food to maintain its ideal condition. The dog food package feeding directions are for the average dog and I have found them more likely aimed for the younger, active dog. One can start by feeding less than recommended and monitor whether to increase or decrease the amounts. There are special diets for weight control, if obesity is an ongoing problem. Another variable is the amount of dog treats given; you may give them as often but decrease the size of the treat. Consult your veterinarian and have him/her make an assessment of your TFT's condition and follow recommendations. Your veterinarian can also rule out medical reasons for obesity.

Finally, an increase in activity is also recommended. Spending more time outdoors in a fenced yard or longer walks via a leash can benefit the dog and owner. We live in a society that finds great pleasure in consuming large quantities of food. It follows then that we want our pets to be equally happy and so we overfeed them. A truer devotion to one's pet, however, reveals itself in concern for the pet's health and longevity.

LEASH TRAINING

You'll want to leash, or lead, train your Toy Fox Terrier. Some people who buy toy dogs make the mistake of not lead training them. They find it easier to just tuck the dog under their arm when they go out. However, there are times when having a leash broken dog is a great convenience. It's safer for your little dog to be on a leash and you'll be able to maintain better control of him. There will also be times when your want your hands free. Of course, if you plan to show your Toy Fox Terrier, leash training is a must.

Most Toy Fox Terriers are easy to leash train. Occasionally, however, one can get a stubborn dog that objects to having anything around his neck. This type of dog can be trained. It will just take a little longer and require more patience. Your dog may be fully lead trained after only one session. A headstrong dog may require a week or more of work.

It is advisable to introduce your TFT to the leash gradually. A lightweight, one piece show lead is best for leash training. Place the leash around your dog's neck. Call his name and talk excitedly to him. Try walking him back and forth. Talk to him all the while, telling him how good he is. You may want to snap your fingers or make little clicking noises. You'll soon learn what is best for keeping your dog's attention. Remember that you must make this fun. If your dog follows you, praise him enthusiastically. Repeat this for a few minutes each day for the next week.

If your dog objects to walking on the leash, you'll have to take the training a little more slowly. Sit down on the floor with your dog. Place the leash on him and spend a few minutes playing with him. Try letting him run around with the leash on. Be sure to keep a close eye on him. You don't want him to get wrapped around the leg of a chair or caught on something. Pick up the end of the lead. Follow the puppy around, holding the lead, while he explores. Stop and encourage the dog to come to you. If he refuses, kneel down and tap your fingers on the floor. This will usually attract his attention and get him to come. Should he still refuse very gently pull him to you. Once he gets to you, pick him up, cuddle him and tell him how wonderful he is for responding. Now, try walking again. If your dog should balk, you'll have to begin all over again. Some headstrong dogs will firmly plant their feet and refuse to move. One occasionally encounters a dog that leaps about like a bucking bronco. He spins in the air and won't keep all four feet on the ground. For this type of dog, persistence is the answer. Just keep giving him short sessions where you make it clear that you expect him to walk. Sooner or later, he will realize that you aren't going to give up.

GROOMING YOUR TFT

The TFT requires only minimal grooming. In fact, this is one of the great advantages of Toy Fox Terrier ownership. This does not mean, however, that grooming is unimportant. Your dog will look and feel better if he's groomed regularly. A dog who is well fed, well cared for and has adequate exercise will usually have a shining, healthy coat. External parasites, such as fleas, can cause the coat to become dry and brittle. Internal parasites (worms) can also wreak havoc with the TFT's coat. Likewise, a dog that is fed a poor diet, particularly one deficient in fat, may have a dry coat. By paying close attention to these factors, however, your TFT's coat will remain lustrous and satiny.

Regular weekly grooming will keep your Toy Fox Terrier looking his best. Frequent grooming will also help to eliminate any doggy odor. Weekly grooming should consist of a thorough brushing with a soft-bristled brush. Begin at the neck and work your way to the tail. If you like, you can follow the brushing with a finger massage. This will help to keep your TFT's skin supple.

You'll also want to inspect your dog's ears when grooming him. Fortunately, with their upright ears, TFTs rarely have ear problems. The inside of the ear can become dirty, though. Clean the ears with a cotton ball or swab. You may wish to moisten the swab with a little alcohol. Under no circumstances should you probe deeper than the eye can see. Occasionally, especially in winter, the ear rims can become dry and cracked. An all-purpose antibiotic/antifungal creme, secured from your veterinarian, and worked into the ear leather, will stem this problem quickly.

Regular inspection of the feet is also beneficial. Look for any sore spots or cracks in the pads. These should be treated promptly. Similarly, burrs or tarry pea gravel can lodge between the pads and cause your pet to limp until removed.

On a monthly basis, you'll want to clip your dog's nails. Some dogs, particularly those kept on rough surfaces, will wear their nails down naturally. Most dogs, however, will need their nails clipped periodically. It's important to keep your dog's nails cut back. Nails which are allowed to grow long will cause the feet to splay. Most breeders use a guillotine-type clipper. Some dogs strongly object to having their nails clipped, and you may want an assistant to help you. It's also sometimes beneficial to shield the dog's eyes so he doesn't see the actual clipping taking place. Try your best to determine exactly where the quick (vein) in the nail ends. This vein is easily seen in dogs with light-colored nails. Take advantage of facing the sun and the veins become clearly visible. For the dark-nailed dog, you'll want to take off only the tip or hook of the nail. Place the nail clipper over the nail and snip the tip off rapidly in a single cut. If you should accidentally cut into the vein, apply a little styptic powder. Each time you clip the dog's nails, the shorter they can be kept.

Toy Fox Terriers rarely need to be bathed. In fact, frequent bathing is not good for the TFT coat as it removes the hair's natural oils. There are some instances, though, when baths are a must. If your TFT has just wallowed in a mud puddle, rolled on something disgusting, or if you're readying him for a show, then a bath is in order. Bathing is essentially the same as for any other dog. Due to the TFT's small size he can generally be bathed in a kitchen or laundry sink. I generally use a wash cloth on the head rather than get excess soap and water in the eyes and ears. A half cotton ball will protect the ear from unwanted moisture. Do be sure to close any nearby windows to prevent chilling. You must protect the dog from drafts until he's completely dry. We dry with towels in moderate weather and use an electric dryer, on medium heat, in cold weather. The dog will be completely dry within minutes. There is a vast array of dog shampoos on the market, and most will work quite well on your dog. I prefer tearless shampoos that enhance the white color. If fleas are a problem in your area, look for a shampoo that kills them. If you find fleas on your dog, be sure to carefully clean the dog's bedding by washing it in hot water and wash the crate.

TEETH

You will want to monitor your puppy's teeth. Those sharp baby teeth usually erupt around the third or fourth week and consist of 28 teeth. From approximately the third month to the sixth month, the 42 permanent teeth erupt. Ideally, the root of the baby tooth is reabsorbed and the permanent tooth pushes it out. In practice, this is often not the case. Perhaps the root of the baby tooth is not totally re-sorbed or the permanent tooth's path does not coincide with the baby tooth. Your veterinarian will want to note if a retained baby tooth deflects the appropriate path of a permanent tooth and will likely sedate the puppy and remove the errant baby tooth. Such a problem could alter your puppy's bite, especially important in a show dog. In my experience, the tooth most often retained is the canine, or fang, tooth. It is often found lodged between the permanent canine and the molar behind it. The good news is that the retained baby canine seldom deflects the permanent canine. The bad news is that it may be wedged tightly and will not loosen on its own, so it will have to be removed.

Like most toy breeds, the Toy Fox Terrier requires constant care of the teeth. Tartar accumulates and hardens, causing gum disease, infected teeth, and the early loss of teeth. We deflect the problem by feeding a dry kibble and offering dog biscuits as rewards. We also offer rawhide chips for the dogs to gnaw. The problem rawhides we have encountered are the small rawhide bones with a knot at each end. As the dog chews and saturates the bone, it becomes soft and soggy and the dog is tempted to swallow the entire bone. I can understand how such rawhides could create intestinal

Chew time. TFTs owned and loved by Deborah J. Hays.

obstructions. We are always vigilant to reclaim a rawhide bone when it reaches a soggy stage. With the rawhide chips, however, the dogs chew on the end of the chip. The chip doesn't disintegrate into a soggy mass like the bones and we retrieve them before they become small enough to swallow whole. We realize that other breeders are vehemently against the use of rawhide and we encourage new owners to follow their breeder's direction and/or to consult their veterinarians for advice. There are a multitude of chewables available at your local pet shop – all created to keep the teeth free of the tartar. Every dog has his own preference and only experimenting with different styles and flavors will reveal the choice most acceptable to the dog and preferred by the breeder.

There are a number of concoctions you can use to clean your dog's teeth. In her excellent book, *Dogs and How to Groom Them*, Hilary Harmar makes several suggestions: "A solution of half and half cold milk and peroxide vol. 10 is excellent for cleaning the teeth, as is a mixture of salt and baking soda moistened sufficiently to form a paste. Human toothpaste can also be used. Dogs do not care for the teeth cleaning operation. It is therefore important to do it gently, quickly, yet thoroughly, and to give great praise afterward. Cleaning your dog's teeth regularly will do much to eliminate the build up of tartar. If your TFT does have a heavy tartar accumulation, you may have to take more drastic measures. Purchase a metal tooth scaler. These are available from many dog supply houses. When scaling teeth, try not to scrape too vigorously. You want to remove the tartar, but you don't want to chip the coat of enamel covering each tooth."

TFTs that are allowed ample chew time should not have to have their teeth cleaned by the vet more than once a year. During this process, your pet will likely be sedated so that each tooth can be cleaned. As the TFT gets older, there may be the need for an extraction, with recovery from an extraction almost instantaneous.

YOUR TFT'S HEALTH

Your TFT will need periodic veterinary visits to safeguard his health. Routine vaccinations will help to protect him. All dogs should be vaccinated, on a yearly basis, for distemper, hepatitis, leptospirosis and parvovirus. You may also wish to have your dog immunized to prevent kennel cough (parainfluenza). Check with your veterinarian to determine if there are any additional diseases prevalent in your region and if a vaccine is available to protect your dog. Thanks to modern vaccines, many highly contagious diseases are almost a thing of the past. Your Toy Fox Terrier will also need a rabies vaccination. Check with your vet to determine how often this should be given. Some states require yearly inoculations while others stipulate that vaccination should be given once every three years.

Make arrangements to have your puppy microchipped by your veterinarian at the first opportunity. A tiny computer chip, encased in a strong, smooth biocompatible glass is injected deep beneath the skin with a syringe. The dog feels no more discomfort than with his routine vaccinations. The chip will last the dog's lifetime and cannot be altered or removed. You will not feel the chip beneath the skin, but a vet clinic or animal shelter with a scanner can detect your dog's unique number and call the manufacturer of the chip for your contact information. No matter how responsible and vigilant the dog owner, a gate left open or a door ajar could allow your pet to get lost. Since more dogs die each year from being lost than die from infectious diseases, it is imperative that your dog be permanently identifiable.

It's a good idea to take your dog to a veterinarian once or twice a year for a general routine examination. Such periodic check-ups will help to detect any problems before they become serious. Take along a stool sample so your vet can examine it microscopically for worms, which can then be treated. Ask your veterinarian if heartworm is prevalent in your area. A simple preventative medication, given daily or monthly, will prevent infestation.

Toy Fox Terriers are a long-lived, healthy breed. Their ancestors on the farms in the early 20th century had to be healthy to survive. There was not much doctoring of animals and especially not farm dogs. Vaccines and antibiotics had not emerged as weapons to fight disease and infection. Survival of the fittest was the code and the farm terriers were rugged, little survivors.

The TFT's early stewardship by the United Kennel Club was another health benefit. The UKC discouraged inbreeding and would stamp the registration papers of

TFT: AmCh/U - Gr Ch. Stonefox Dragon Heart.
Dobe: U-Gr Ch. Stonefox Mortal Combat, CGC TDI, SD.
Both owned by Karen Brancheau. Photo by Mary Bloom.

inbred dogs. The result was that many of the genetic diseases that have appeared in other breeds did not find their way into the TFT gene pool. This gene pool, bolstered by out-crossing, was slow to set type, but created a breed that could live 15-20 years without the heritable problems of other breeds.

Breeders tended to keep their older dogs rather than placing them after prime breeding ages. By keeping the older dogs, breeders were aware of health problems that might occur and were able to adjust their breeding program accordingly. The little dog who completed his titles and held up physically till the age of 16 was a TFT to build a breeding program around.

Between 1999 through 2004, several heritable conditions have been identified that may express themselves in the TFT. These conditions may have always existed, but breeders were not able to label the conditions. No statistics are available on the prevalence of these conditions and research is being conducted.at the present time. A brief description of these conditions follows.

Congenital Hypothyroidism with Goiter (CHG)

This is a disease that afflicts newborn puppies. Such puppies are born with large heads and appear lethargic. Many die prior to three weeks, their eyes still closed, their coat coarse, the ear canals small, and they do not grow. A swelling under the neck develops by the second week and begins to grow. If correctly diagnosed, the administration of thyroid hormone will stop all of the effects with the exception of the goiter. However, this goiter will eventually interfere with breathing. It is known that the availability of thyroid hormone is crucial to rapidly growing puppies. CHG puppies are unable to produce this thyroid hormone.

CHG manifests itself when both parents of the litter possess this recessive trait, presenting about 25% of their progeny with the disease. Another 25% will carry the recessive gene and continue the disease if mated to another carrier. The rest of the puppies will remain normal.

Dr. John C. Fyfe was instrumental in identifying the genetic basis of this disease and eventually offering testing for it through the Laboratory of Comparative Medical Genetics at Michigan State University. A blood sample may be tested to identify whether a TFT's DNA carries the recessive trait. This test allows carriers to be identified and thus eliminated from breeding programs.

Von Willebrand's Disease (vWD)

This is a bleeding disorder that is usually exhibited in a mild form. Most dogs exhibit symptoms infrequently enough to allow a normal existence. Dogs with vWD may experience nosebleeds, blood in urine or stool, or bleeding from the gums. Females may bleed profusely while in season or at whelping. Fading puppies may signify that vWD is present, with both parents carriers and the puppies born dead or fading shortly after birth. Excessive bleeding during surgery may be the first alert that your pet has this problem.

The formation of blood platelets is vital to the coagulation process. The von Willebrand factor (vWF) encourages cell platelets to do their job in stopping the bleeding. If the amount of this factor is reduced bleeding is prolonged. There are several breeds for which this disease is so prevalent that genetic tests are available to locate carriers. For most other breeds, including the TFT, carriers can be identified with a blood test for von Willebrand factor.

Although most breeds encounter the milder form of vWD called Type I, there are two more serious varieties—Type II and Type III. Bleeding is severe in both as levels of vWF are lowered. In Type III, the affected dogs have zero levels of vWF. Fortunately, Type II and III are rare.

Legg-Calve-Perthe (LCP)

Although the TFT is not identified by the Orthopedic Foundation of America (OFA) as one of the breeds at risk for LCP, many toy and terrier breeds are mentioned. It behooves TFT breeders to be vigilant lest the condition ravage the breed.

This disorder is most likely to occur between the age of four months to one year. It evolves as the blood supply is interrupted to the femur (the thighbone), causing bone cells to die. To compensate, a new blood supply is generated to build new bone cells, but results in an irregular fit of the head of the femur into the pelvic socket. The dog loses flexibility in the rear and experiences pain.

The exact manner in which this disorder is inherited is unknown at this time. Common sense would dictate that afflicted animals should not be used for breeding.

Patellar Luxation or Slipped Stifles

Have you ever dislocated a knee, shoulder or finger? Have you ever had your back go out on you and had to carefully maneuver it back into place? If you've experienced any of these painful predicaments, then you have some sense of how a dog might feel with slipped stifles (knees). The patella is analogous to the human kneecap.

This canine knee is a bony structure that fits in a groove (trochlea) at the lower end of the femur (thighbone). It is held in place by raised lips on either side of the trochlea as well as by strong ligaments. If these lips or ridges are not sufficiently developed, the knee cap will leave its normal position and rest either on the inside of the inner lip (medial dislocation) or on the outside of the outer lip (lateral dislocation). Medial dislocations can be graded from grade one, a mild form generally not needing surgery, to grade four, a severe form in which the patella is dislocated all the time and requires surgery.

The disease can certainly be attributed to heredity. Breeders who retain their senior TFTs would be very aware should this problem occur in their lines. Breeders also can have their veterinarian examine breeding stock for the problem and eliminate those afflicted from the breeding program. However, just as accidents or falls can trigger dislocations in humans, active young dogs may also injure themselves resulting in a dislocation.

Demodectic Mange

Most cases of demodectic mange are noted in young puppies still nursing their mother. As a matter of fact, the demodex mite, which lives at the base of a strand of hair, is transferred to the puppies within the first week of life. The small areas of hair loss are most often about the head and front feet, both of which are in constant contact with the dam during nursing.

The transfer of these mites is not unusual, because virtually every adult dog has them without any apparent symptoms being noted. The immune system of adults and most puppies are able to withstand the infestation of mites. Those puppies that suffer hair loss and skin irritation have immune systems that are deficient or may not be developed enough to deal with the mites. The latter may literally grow out of the problem as the immune system develops. However, puppy owners should consult their veterinarian when their puppies experience this hair loss. The veterinarian will scrape the irritated skin to check for the mites, which can be seen via microscope. The vet may recommend a topical cream or dip. Such treatment is successful most of the time and the dog never suffers infection again.

In a small number of cases, larger areas of hair loss cover not only the head and front feet, but also the neck and torso. This more serious condition can result in crusty, oozing lesions. The dog may experience an elevated temperature and become depressed and listless. Multiple dips and drug therapy will eventually make the dog right, but treatment here may be a matter of months rather than weeks.

An immune system that allows this condition to occur should obviously not be replicated. Dogs that suffer from demodectic mange to any degree should be spayed or neutered.

Progressive Retinal Atrophy

This inherited disease of the eye leads to the deterioration of the retina. It manifests itself in different forms that can appear in puppies a few weeks old up to varying ages of adults. Most owners are unaware of their pet's declining sight due to the canine's heightened sense of smell and hearing. In familiar surroundings, the symptoms may be difficult to identify until the disease is advanced. Difficulty seeing at night is generally the first sign for the dog's owner that something is amiss. The speed of progression may differ, but most affected dogs become completely blind eventually.

There is no cure for this disease, but obviously animals affected and their parents should not be bred again. A veterinarian can identify the disease through examination with an ophthalmoscope. There is no quantification of TFTs affected at this time as there is in other breeds where the condition has decimated breed stock and DNA testing is available. The TFT has been the result of out cross breeding up to the present. However, as breeders do more close-up breeding, the opportunity for this disease to appear will be greater. Like many diseases where recessive genes carry the disorder, carriers mated with normal dogs will not produce the disease, but produce more carriers. As breedings become concentrated within families, the chances of carrier being bred to carrier increase. A winning dog produced in this manner may be used by eager breeders who discover down the line that the stud is propagating the disease.

CONCLUSION

Even though I am unable to substantiate the exact degree of involvement for the TFT in each of these six conditions, anecdotal evidence tells me that some TFTs have experienced such problems. Since heredity plays a role in each, the responsible breeder will want to screen breeding stock, follow the development of said stock throughout their life cycle, and seek feedback from puppy buyers about any problems that may occur in a puppy's lifetime. The average TFT owner will never experience any of these six conditions. This information is offered so that breeders and pet owners can remain vigilant with the goal of eliminating these problems from the gene pool.

THE STUD DOG

Great care should be taken in the selection of a stud dog. Whether you are purchasing a male for your own use or are planning to pay a fee for the use of an outside dog, much thought should go into the choice. The male Toy Fox Terrier can have a tremendous impact on the breed. While a female will have only one litter a year, a male can be bred many, many times. He can pass on his good qualities, as well as his faults, to a great number of offspring. Indeed, a very popular stud, used for many years, can have a far-reaching impact on the breed. While it is admittedly more convenient to purchase a stud for your kennel, it may not be the wisest strategic move. You will be bound to this one male largely because of convenience. Without him, you would be shipping your females to various destinations or purchasing semen from a variety of studs with a variety of bloodlines. If the stud you purchase sires mediocre puppies or frequently misses on his breedings, you have invested considerable money, time, and effort with little compensation.

What should you look for in a stud dog? Above all, he should be an outstanding representative of the breed. The stud should be a conformation champion – perhaps in both AKC and UKC registries. You might look for a stud who excels in areas you wish to improve in your breeding stock. For example, if you are not pleased with the correctness of fronts on your TFT, don't settle for anything other than a perfect front on your stud.

Offering a stud to the public for breeding can be awkward. Will you be able to tell someone that his or her bitch is not a good enough specimen to be bred and turn down the fee? Are you prepared to board females for a week or two and be responsible for their health and well being? How will your stud contract read? How much will you charge? How many repeat breedings will be offered in the event the breeding results in no puppies? What if only one puppy results from the breeding? Will you consider trading the service for your choice of a puppy? How will you deal with those who blame your stud for the poor qualities of the litter? Expectations will be high that every puppy will be show quality.

Ch. Shirleydjazz Platium Crown Baron winning Best of Breed under Dr. John Davidson. Photo by Alverson Photographers, Inc.

Pedigree is of great importance when you're deciding on a stud. The pedigree should reflect a background of careful breeding. Since the stud dog passes on the qualities transmitted to him by his ancestors, it will help if you can learn as much as possible about the dogs named in the pedigree. Look for a balanced breeding, with champion dogs on both sides of the stud's pedigree. It may be tempting to use a dog sired by "Grand Champion Mr. Wonderful", but if his mother was "Little Miss I Have Every Fault" then you are just as likely to get puppies resembling the grandmother as you are Mr. Wonderful. You might note if Grand Champion Mr. Wonderful is in the pedigree more than once—perhaps on both the sire and dam's side of the pedigree.

The real proof of the pudding with a stud dog is how well he can produce. The effectiveness of a stud dog should be measured by the quality of his progeny. It's a sad fact of life that some spectacular show winners never sire progeny as good as themselves. Conversely, some less flashy dogs may consistently produce outstanding offspring. If you are using an outside stud, try to obtain as much information as possible about the quality of the Toy Fox Terriers he has produced. If you are using one of your own studs, keep detailed records and photos of his offspring. Check back with puppy buyers and try to see (in person or in photos) how the puppies matured. This way you will be able to see if your dog is living up to his potential as a stud.

While physical qualities are undeniably important, don't forget to look for a dog that excels in temperament. A dog passes on not only his conformation, but also his personality. A TFT who is shy and sluggish or overly aggressive is not typical and makes an unsuitable stud dog. You must remember that the majority of your puppies will probably enter pet homes, where temperament will be of prime importance.

Last, but certainly not least, you want a dog that is healthy and vigorous. It's best if he comes from a background of long-lived, healthy dogs. If you are offering your dog for public stud, or purchasing from another breeder, you will want to have him tested and cleared for major health concerns as outlined in the chapter Caring for Your TFT.

You also want a dog that is a reliable breeder. While a dog's reliability as a stud is often molded by his early breeding experiences, the dog that is uniformly healthy and hardy is most likely to consistently have a good sperm count. Bitches bred to such a vigorous dog are more likely to become pregnant and deliver strong puppies.

All breeders hope that they will have a pre-potent stud. This is a male who is dominant for his virtues and can overcome the faults of most bitches. He can be used with success on a wide variety of bitches. Such studs can quickly make a name for a kennel and contribute much to its success. You are indeed fortunate if you discover that you own such a dog. A truly pre-potent male comes along rarely, so take advantage of him if you are lucky enough to own one. Don't hesitate to seek the services of a pre-potent stud owned by another breeder.

RAISING THE STUD DOG

Experienced breeders have learned that healthy, hardy dogs are most likely to be active, vigorous studs. A good, well-balanced diet, coupled with plenty of exercise, is important for the stud dog. You want him in top-notch condition. Be sure to check for both internal and external parasites. Worms and fleas will sap his energy, and a male in run down condition may well have a below normal sperm count.

The mental attitude of a stud dog is important. You want a lively, confident dog that is sure of himself and enthusiastic about breeding. Therefore, he must be handled differently than a pet male. At an early age, your male dog will begin to mount and ride other dogs. Do not be upset if you find him trying to mount other males. He may even latch on to your leg and thrust enthusiastically. While it would be acceptable to chastise a pet male, you'll have to be more tolerant with the future stud dog. Repeatedly telling him "No" at an early age may discourage him. You don't want to convey the impression that breeding is wrong. If he becomes too much of a nuisance, separate him from the other dogs. If he's riding your leg, you might try distracting his attention with a favorite toy, or take him out for a walk.

If at all possible, you'll want to breed your dog for the first time while he's still young. Many breeders find twelve months an ideal age to begin. All TFTs are individuals, though, and an occasional male will take longer to become interested in breeding. Once a male has sired his first litter, he is referred to as a proven stud.

That first breeding is very important. You want everything to go well, as this experience will set the tone for future breedings. Take the time to observe your dog's actions closely. You will see how he responds to females in season and how he

AKC CH UKC Gr. Ch. Meadowood's Buster Brown owned by John and Sally Davidson. Photo by Ken Schwab.

approaches the mating process. You will also be training your dog to be the type of stud you want. He will learn to respond to your encouragement. You will aid him by holding the bitch so that he can breed her successfully and efficiently, and you will both learn to function together as a team. While it will take time and patience to accomplish this, you will find that the time is well spent, as you will end up with the type of reliable and eager stud you can always count on.

It's best if your dog's first breeding is to a proven, easily bred bitch. Working with two inexperienced dogs can try the patience of the most experienced breeder. The maiden bitch is likely to flirt and to sit down when the male tries to mount her. Even worse, she may snap at him as he mounts. While some dogs will ignore this, it could confuse and discourage your inexperienced male, and spoil his enthusiasm for breeding. If you have little experience yourself and you must breed two unproven dogs, then it might be wise to obtain the help of an experienced breeder.

The inexperienced male is more apt to flirt and play with the female. Some of this should be permitted for it will increase his excitement. However, you don't want him to get into the habit of playing excessively. You want him to attend to the business at hand. Verbally encourage him. You don't want to talk so much that you distract him, but you do want to let him know that you approve of what he's doing. No matter how frustrated you become, don't lose your patience. This could ruin the dog for future breeding. Take your time and don't hurry him. He'll soon have the idea.

Some breeders simply put the male and female in a run and leave them alone for several days hoping that they will breed. This is an inefficient and dangerous way of handling breeding. They have no idea if or precisely when the female was bred. This makes it difficult to plan for the whelping. If you are controlling the breeding and for some reason the stud will not service the bitch, all is not lost. You may still have time to try another stud with the bitch. Be aware that accidents do occasionally happen and either the bitch or, more likely, the stud could be injured. By controlling the breeding you will be able to minimize the risk of injury.

It's best to teach your stud dog that you will hold the bitch for him. Some males, particularly those who've bred on their own previously, will have nothing to do with a female if you insist on holding her. This can lead to problems when you try him with a difficult bitch. If you are breeding a small stud to a larger female, you may have to reposition the dogs so they can breed successfully. A male who will not allow you to assist will be annoying. Encourage the stud to mount the bitch while you hold her. Avoid talking too much when he's attempting to actually penetrate her. After he's tied, you may indeed pet him and tell him how pleased you are with the job he's done. This way he will learn to be comfortable with having you touch him during the breeding process.

A good stud can continue to sire puppies into his old age. After the age of eight to ten years, however, you may note that some of the bitches he has bred do not conceive. His fertility may diminish during hot weather, for instance. If you're not ready to permanently retire your still valuable stud, you may wish to arrange for periodic sperm counts to be taken.

HANDLING THE MATING

You may want to allow the dogs to become familiar with each other before the breeding. Some owners place the dogs in adjacent runs so that they can become acquainted. In larger breeds, it often takes two people to handle the breeding. With the small Toy Fox Terrier, however, it's possible for one person to control both the dog and the bitch. If you are uncertain, placing a leash on the bitch will give you added control.

Take a few moments to plan for the breeding before you bring out both dogs. You'll want to do the breeding in a small area where the dogs will be free from distraction. It's best if the stud is familiar with the area, so that he will feel comfortable. You want a surface where your male will have good footing. If you'll be breeding the dogs in the house, you may want to spread out a piece of old carpeting. If your stud is smaller than the bitch, you might want to have a small rug on hand. This can be folded so that he can stand on it and elevate his height.

Be sure to prepare for your own comfort, too. Once the male penetrates the female, his penis will swell and the dogs will become tied together. A tie may last only a few minutes or it could continue for an hour. Most ties last between 15 – 25 minutes. Try to make yourself as comfortable as you can. If you find a position where you're able to rest your back against a wall, you may be more comfortable. You don't want to be distracted either. If you're expecting an important phone call, try to move the telephone within reach.

If you wish you may allow the dogs to play and flirt for a few minutes. Sit down on the floor near the dogs and keep a hand on the bitch. Hold her firmly with your hand on her shoulders or gently encircling her neck. After some initial nuzzling and licking, your male will probably start licking the bitch's vulva. If she's ready to be bred, she'll raise her tail and elevate her vulva. The male will then usually mount her. You'll have to be prepared to control the bitch if she starts to snap or tries to sit or lie down. You'll want to try to line up the bitch and the stud. If he is out of position, very gently push him away and encourage him to try again. You will most likely be able to tell when the male has penetrated by the reaction of the bitch. Just make sure she stands solidly on all four feet until he stops thrusting. Once he's stopped, look closely and make sure the dogs are properly tied. If you see the swollen bulb of the penis outside the vagina, you have an outside tie and you'll have to handle this somewhat differently from the normal tie. Assuming that this is a normal breeding, your stud dog will probably slide his front feet off the bitch's back. You may notice that he is anxious to turn. Gently help him bring his hind leg over the bitch's back. Both dogs will then be standing tail to tail. If, while he's turning, your male should cry out in pain, quickly bring him back to the original position. You don't want to take the chance of injuring him.

Just when you think your back will break and your legs have gone permanently to sleep, the dogs will separate. It may take you a few seconds to realize that they are no longer linked. Some breeders like to hold the bitch's hindquarters up in the air for a few seconds to avoid losing any sperm. Others consider this a waste of time.

It's best to separate the dogs once they have separated from a tie. Some terrifically enthusiastic stud dogs will mount the bitch and attempt to breed again. Give the dogs some fresh water and allow them to rest. Most breeders skip a day and then breed once more on the following day.

Following the breeding, stud dog owners should keep an eye on their dogs. Most males will retract the penis into the sheath shortly after the breeding has taken place. Occasionally, however, the tip of the penis remains red and swollen and doesn't settle back properly into the sheath. This can usually be corrected by grasping the sheath and

gently massaging it by pulling and pushing toward the end of the penis. In most cases, this will force the penis to retract. If this problem occurs, be sure to check the dog frequently to make sure that the penis remains in the sheath. On rare occasions, it will be necessary to use a lubricant on the swollen penis to get it back into the sheath.

Ch. Meadowwood's Rocky Top owned by John and Sally Davidson.

THE OUTSIDE TIE

An outside tie occurs when the bulb, located at the rear of a dog's penis, swells outside the bitch's vagina. An outside tie is more difficult for the inexperienced breeder to handle. Nevertheless, while less desirable than an inside tie, a properly handled outside tie is often successful. Some males seem more prone to outside ties, and, while they are more trouble to breed, they can and do sire puppies.

With an outside tie, it is best to hold the penis behind the swollen bulb. Place your other hand on the bitch's belly and press her backwards. You can allow the stud to turn, but it's usually easier to keep the pair linked if he remains mounted. You'll want to hold the bitch and stud together as long as possible. Though the dogs may be restless, try to keep them together for at least five minutes.

THE RELUCTANT STUD

Most Toy Fox Terriers are eager and reliable studs. Sometimes, however, despite the best of training, you'll encounter a lackadaisical stud. Such males try the patience of breeders. There will be times, despite everything you try, when you simply can't achieve a successful breeding. You'll have to decide whether you want to work with this type of stud. If he's already produced outstanding puppies or is the only male to carry on your line, then it may be worth the effort.

The reluctant stud usually flirts and plays with the bitch until he's exhausted. He seems unable to concentrate on the breeding and rapidly loses interest. You'll have to devise your own methods of dealing with the reluctant stud. Your main objective will be to perk him up and excite him. You must be inventive and extra encouraging with this type of stud. Giving in to the frustration you are bound to feel, by yelling at him, will cause the reluctant male to quit.

Try short breeding sessions for the hesitant stud. If a breeding isn't accomplished in a short amount of time, stop. Let him calm down and relax. Try again in an hour or two. If he seems intent on playing and won't respond to your encouragement, there are a few things you might try. Standup, gather the bitch into your arms and announce that you're taking her away. If he jumps around excitedly, try once again. You might well be successful. You can also try placing the female in a crate. The male will probably circle the crate, dancing about, whining and barking. The female he showed no interest in previously now seems terribly attractive to him. If he seems truly excited, take the bitch from the crate and try again. If, however, he lies quietly down and shows no interest, you have little chance of a successful breeding.

AKC CH UKC Gr. Ch. Jacobs and Chestnuts Struten His Stuf "Strut" bred by Dorothy Jacobs. Owned by Mark and Judy Threlfall. Exhibited by Judy Chestnut Threlfall. Photo by Susan Booth.

Sometimes jealousy can be used to excite the reluctant stud. Place the male in a crate and bring out another stud. Allow him to watch as the male flirts and attempts to breed the bitch. Of course, you must pay close attention or you are likely to get a breeding you don't want! Even the most disinterested of studs usually gets his ire up over the sight of a rival male with *his* bitch. When you feel that he's sufficiently fired up, remove the opposing male. Your stud, now eager and excited, can be released from his crate and will often consummate the breeding.

By carefully raising your male TFT and handling his first few matings successfully, you will be well on your way to owning a reliable stud dog. With encouragement and sensible guidance, your dog will quickly learn what's expected of him. From experience, you will discover how best to handle him. And, hopefully, he'll produce many champions for you!

ARTIFICIAL INSEMINATION

With the help of your veterinarian, successful breeding can be accomplished despite the reluctance of the stud or bitch. You may wish to have the vet monitor the bitch's season to assure the optimum breeding times. Most females, however, will flag their tail and lift the vulva to signal when they are ready to breed. The veterinarian will manually work the stud to engorgement while using the scent of the female to entice him. The collected semen will be checked for viability and then immediately injected via tubing into the female. You will likely return in two days for another session. Note that the verification form signed by the vet will have to be included with registration papers on the resultant puppies.

There are breeders who will ship fresh or frozen semen for injection into the female. Involve your vet if you decide to engage in this type of artificial insemination.

THE BROOD BITCH

SHOULD YOU BREED YOUR TOY FOX TERRIER?

You love your Toy Fox Terrier and she amazes everyone with her intelligence and delights them with her personality. "If you ever breed that dog, I'd like to have a pup," they tell you. "Hmm," you think, "That might be fun, we could keep a pup, and make a few bucks also." I can't tell you how many times I have heard this scenario. The new breeder starts calling around for stud service or wishes to purchase a male. I generally invite them out for a visit to evaluate their female. Almost universally, the bitch will not be breeding quality and her pedigree is undistinguished. I tell them that the purpose of breeding is to improve the breed- to breed the best specimens as ascertained by judges at dog shows. This generally falls on deaf ears, as it seems to them that perhaps we breeders don't want the competition. Just looking at Nippy they know that she's the best looking dog ever!

What does have impact, however, is when I start enumerating the costs associated with a typical breeding, from stud service through weaning. And those costs are only if all goes well and a cesarean section is not needed or extra vet care is not needed for the puppies. Now divide those costs by the 2 or 3 puppies your female is likely to whelp. The math reveals that it is actually cheaper to buy a puppy from a breeder. Those relatives or neighbors who wanted a pup out of your female may not be willing to pay several hundred dollars for a puppy when what they really hoped was that you would give them a puppy!

Finally, I emphasize that gestating and whelping a litter is a dangerous process and that I have lost females for various reasons during this process. I ask if they are really willing to put this wonderful little pet in harm's way just to make a few puppy sales. Do they have the time and energy to get up every three hours to feed a weak puppy or stay up all night whelping a litter and report to work the following day?

The logical conclusion is to spay her and allow her to live a long life as a treasured companion.

This beauty is Gr. Ch. "PR" Meadowood's Ms. Melody, owned by John Davidson, of Dunlap, Illinois.

I invite these folks to attend an upcoming dog show and to watch the breed being evaluated. I tell them to visit other breeders in the state. If they are still interested at that point, I encourage them to reserve the best bitch puppy they can find and exhibit it. Then, perhaps in two year's time, we can talk about breeding. If these points are made in a gentle manner, fledging breeders might persevere and get involved in the breed. We do a disservice when we dismiss them outright- how many successful breeders today started the same way? Treated rudely, they will continue to look for a male to prove you wrong and they will find a backyard breeder somewhere to accommodate them.

Breeding dogs requires a significant investment. The cost of a good dog is only part of this investment. Calculate the cost of equipment, veterinary costs, food, and dog shows. The actual price of the dog pales beside these associated costs. Yet many of us must find it rewarding despite the bite out of our wallet. It is a great hobby for a family to pursue, but should one be less than totally committed, you might want to reevaluate.

I am assuming since you have purchased this breed book, that you are one of those who enter the world of breeding with the goal of improving the breed. I know you understand that you will seldom break even and that there will be as many downs as ups. You do this because you love dogs and nothing will ever replace the thrill of finishing your own homebred champion.

THE BROOD BITCH

Much of what we've said about stud dog selection applies equally to the brood bitch. The beginning breeder will make no more important selection than the purchase of a good brood bitch. The strength of your breeding program will be based on your continuing production of good bitches. While many breeders make a grand

Pipi owned by Marsha Shively. Dam of the year in 1999.

splash with a sensational winning dog, the true breeder knows that a line of top-producing bitches is his ticket to success. Excellent brood bitches form the cornerstone of the carefully planned breeding program. If you are using outside studs and a breeding proves unsuccessful, it's relatively easy to change course. If, however, your female is unsuitable as a brood bitch, you must either begin again or be plagued with years of trying to breed up from a mediocre start. The brood bitch is the rock upon which the foundation of your kennel will rest. Selection of the appropriate brood bitch, therefore, is essential.

The brood bitch does not necessarily have to be a champion herself. Her phenotype, however, should be just as good. In fact, she may be available because she doesn't enjoy the show ring. It may prove difficult to purchase a brood bitch, as the serious breeder is loath to let a good one get away. Be patient. Get to know the breeders you most respect and win their confidence. You may be presented with an offer for co-ownership, if the breeder wishes to play a role in future breedings. A contract will be presented which you should study carefully and fully understand before you sign. It is imperative that she is carefully bred and from a line that has a reputation for producing consistent quality. After reviewing the standard carefully, decide which qualities are most important to you. Select a bitch from a line that excels in those virtues. Look for a bitch who is structurally sound and one that excels in temperament. You'll be on your way to producing Toy Fox Terriers of which you can be proud.

BREEDING SIZE

If you are thinking of breeding your Toy Fox Terrier bitch, then size is an important consideration. Whether you use weight or height as the criterion for size, always gravitate to the medium size bitch. I look for sturdy bitches that aren't overly narrow in the hips and pelvis. By following these guidelines, I've been able to minimize whelping difficulties and keep Caesarian sections to a minimum.

Some owners prefer tiny Toy Fox Terriers. Such bitches, however, are questionable candidates for breeding. Breeding a TFT bitch of less than 4 pounds can be extremely dangerous. Most tiny bitches simply aren't as capable of delivering their puppies naturally. The puppies may not take after the dam and may be too large for natural delivery. A Caesarian section is often necessary for these little bitches. Administering anesthesia to any dog is risky, but it's especially perilous with tiny bitches. Make no mistake about it, a Caesarian section is stressful. Think long and hard before breeding the very small TFT bitch. You could well lose both the mother and her puppies.

While most Toy Fox Terrier bitches whelp easily and naturally, some do require Caesarians. Normal size females may require a C-section under certain conditions. Generally this occurs when there is an overly large puppy, a dead puppy or a puppy that mal-presents. Problem puppies such as these can block the birth canal. Unlike larger breeds, there is not much room to maneuver a TFT puppy obstructing the canal. Many bitches who, because of these problems, require a C-section can later go on to whelp litters naturally.

Controversy abounds over whether bitches that routinely require Caesarians should be included in a breeding program. No breeder really likes C-sections. They are expensive, stressful to both the mother and the pups, and very inconvenient. For some perverse reason, it seems that bitches requiring Caesarians never go into labor until two or three in the morning.

Each breeder will have to decide whether it is worth including bitches requiring routine Caesarians in their breeding program. Much will depend on the quality of the bitch and litters she produces. If she have already produced a litter of outstanding quality, you will doubtless grant her more latitude. If the C-section was due to an overly large puppy, a dead pup, or a difficult presentation, you may try breeding the bitch again. If the bitch requires successive Caesarians, you must decide if it is worth continuing to breed her. Some breeders accept C-sections as a way of life and anticipate them. Other breeders feel that the best way to insure a line of natural-whelping bitches is to eliminate those requiring Caesarian sections from their breeding program, regardless of the quality of the litters they produce.

Breeders are often faced with the dilemma of whether to breed oversized bitches. It is always a temptation, as these larger bitches may be of excellent type, often produce larger litters, and usually whelp easily. They may or may not replicate their large size in their offspring. You will have the opportunity to select the medium sized puppies in the litter, offering the larger puppies as pets. Many owners of large bitches try to mitigate the problem by breeding to tiny studs. What they don't realize is that the puppies will still inherit the genes for size. They are likely to find in their litter a lovely oversized male and a tiny bitch. If you opt to breed a large bitch, search for a properly sized male who comes from a long line of properly sized TFTs. If you can find such a male with a history of producing moderate sized offspring, you will be better off. Don't be tempted into thinking that the male, just because he's small, will necessarily produce small sized puppies.

BREEDING AGE

Toy Fox Terrier females generally come in season for the first time between eight and eleven months of age. The majority of birches in my kennel begin their seasons at nine to ten months. All TFTs are individuals, however, and occasionally you will find bitches that come into season at seven months, as well as some that wait until they are almost a year old.

Most books will tell you that bitches come into season every six months. It appears, however, that most Toy Fox Terriers haven't read these books! Most TFT females come into season every seven to eight months. I have had a few that did come into season every six months and some at longer intervals. We have noticed that one female in season in the kennel tends to bring other females in season. Once in awhile, I have also had a rare female who had only one season per year.

Your female will need time to grow and mature before being bred. She must be ready, not only physically, but also emotionally and mentally, for the task of having puppies. Wait until the second season to breed your bitch. This should allow her to mature without the stress of whelping a litter. Furthermore, many TFT bitches have an incomplete first season and will fail to conceive. Under no circumstances should any bitch, no matter how large she may be, be bred so that she'll have a litter before she is one year old.

Most breeders prefer to breed their bitches, for the first time, before they reach the age of three. Certainly bitches can and do whelp successfully for the first time after three years of age. Very often, however, it is more difficult for these older bitches to conceive. Like the very young bitch, the older maiden bitch may encounter difficulties in whelping.

Novices often ask when a bitch is too old for breeding. This is difficult to answer. Breeders frequently continue to breed their bitches into their eighth year. Much depends on the health and condition of the bitch, and how many times she has been bred. If she has only been bred 2 or 3 times, it is likely she can be bred successfully. Frequently older bitches are

Ch. "PR" Currens' Suzy Jr. of Parkside was the first champion from Howard and Doris Currens' illustrious Parkside Kennels, in Port Huron, Michigan.

less regular in their seasons than younger bitches. You should be aware that older bitch-es are also more prone to complications during whelping, and a Caesarian may be nec-essary. Still, if you want one last litter from your fabulous brood bitch and she is still in good condition, you can try. I have known of a bitch as old as eleven years of age that produced a litter.

Most breeders breed their brood bitches one season, then skip the next season. This allows the bitch to recover fully and replenish her resources, in preparation for her next litter. There is nothing that grieves the dog lover quite as much as seeing a bitch bred successively season after season until she wears out. If you have a bitch, that comes into season every ten or 12 months, however, it is permissible to breed her every season. If you feel compelled to breed your bitch on successive seasons, then do allow her to rest on her third heat cycle. Above all, let common sense be your guide. If your brood bitch has a litter of one or two puppies and raises them without difficulty, it might not be too much of a strain to breed on her next season. If, however, she has just finished raising a litter of five, you are asking a great deal to expect her to raise another litter on her next season.

CONDITIONING THE FUTURE MOM

The best time to begin conditioning the brood bitch is before she is bred. Your best bet for ensuring vigorous, strong puppies and few whelping problems, is to start with a bitch in tip-top condition. Now is the perfect time for a routine veterinary visit. A fecal examination should be done to detect the presence of worms. It is best to have your bitch treated now, before she's bred. You'll also want to be sure she is up-to-date on her yearly vaccinations. Have the vet attend promptly to any vaginal infections. Immediate treatment is in order for any skin conditions that the bitch might transmit to the puppies.

Now is also the time to stop for a moment and take a long look at the future mom's physique. You want to have her in good, hard condition. A flabby, overweight bitch may have difficulty becoming pregnant and delivering her litter should she become pregnant. Excess weight interferes with effective contractions. Similarly, the thin underweight bitch is apt to be dragged down by the burden of a litter and may have difficulty maintaining her milk. Now, not after breeding, is the best time to achieve the ideal weight. We use a general guide of not wanting to see ribs, but want-ing to easily feel ribs when we pick the female up. We also want to see a nice tuck up before breeding our bitch.

Optimum muscle tone is also important. A bitch whose muscles are in tight, hard condition is likely to have fewer complications. It is usually not difficult to get

*Gr. Ch. "PR" Bay Toys Noel of Windy Acres is
one of the fine brood bitches from Loren and
Shirley Stroud's Windy Acres Kennel, in Victoria,
Texas.*

Toy Fox Terriers to exercise. Thankfully, ours is
a lively, energetic breed. Still, make sure your
bitch gets sufficient exercise. You want her in
the peak of condition. Exercise can be especially useful in helping to trim the figure of an
overweight bitch. If your Toy Fox Terrier bitch
would rather relax on the sofa, you will have to encourage her to exercise. Toss a ball
or a Frisbee, or take her for a daily walk. While she may be reluctant to exercise on
her own, chances are she will be delighted at the prospect of spending some time
with you. She will feel better and you will feel more confident in breeding her.

COORDINATING WITH THE STUD DOG OWNER

Contact the owner of the stud you have selected as soon as your bitch begins
her season. There is nothing as frustrating, to a stud owner, as receiving a frantic
telephone call announcing a bitch must be bred immediately. Stud dog owners have
busy lives, too. Courtesy and thoughtfulness will go a long way toward friendly rela-
tions. If you aren't certain of the exact day your bitch's season began, let the stud
dog's owner know. He can arrange for you to deliver the bitch a few days early.

UNDERSTANDING YOUR BITCH'S SEASON

It is an aid to breeders to have a basic understanding of their female's heat, or
estrus, cycle. If we have a general grasp of how the bitch's body functions during the
breeding season, it will make it easier to determine the optimum days for breeding.
Your bitch will be in season for approximately eighteen to twenty-one days.
Young bitches may, for the first estrus, have an immature, or incomplete, season of
shorter duration. It is easy to miss the first few days of a bitch's season, so close attention is essential. Your first indication that your bitch is in season will likely be the
sight of a few drops of blood. You will also note that her vulva swells, although at this
early stage it will feel firm when touched. Some bitches are quite adept at keeping

themselves clean. If you suspect that your bitch is in season, you may want to line her kennel or crate with a white cloth (an old sheet or white towel is ideal) so that you will be able to confirm your suspicions. Some bitches have a pinkish discharge, but most show bright red blood.

During this first phase, you may notice behavioral changes in your TFT female. Some bitches become anxious and nervous, while others seem overly affectionate. A bitch may be a bit testy with other females. Don't be surprised if she needs to go out to relieve herself more than usual. These changes are due to the sudden production of hormones and are quite normal. This first phase of your bitch's season will last approximately one week. You should be aware, however, that all Toy Fox Terrier bitches are individuals and many vary from this general guideline.

The second phase of the season is the one that most concerns breeders. It is during this time that the bitch is ready to be bred. By this time, your bitch's vaginal secretion will have changed. Most likely it will become clear or take on a yellowish tinge (breeders often refer to this as "straw-colored"). A light touch of your bitch's vulva, with a piece of toilet paper, will generally show greater swelling. It will be softer and almost flabby in nature. The vaginal opening will be more prominent.

The bitch's demeanor will definitely change during the second phase. She will flirt eagerly with other dogs. If you have her in an enclosure with other bitches, you may find that they are mounting her. Some females become quite brazen in their flirtations. Owners must exercise caution during this phase of the bitch's cycle. Not only is the bitch intensely interested in being bred, but also she is extremely enticing to males. The odor of her urine will proclaim to every male that she is available. Indeed, you may find a pack of males camped out on your front lawn.

Watch closely for your bitch to exhibit the classic, telltale sign of breeding readiness…flagging her tail. She will raise her tail and flip it slightly to the side. She will also elevate her vulva in anticipation. It is best to breed a couple of days after the bitch begins flagging her tail. This is usually on the tenth to the thirteenth day. Treat this on an individual basis. Let the bitch's behavior be your guide. Most breeders breed one day, skip a day, and then repeat the breeding. This increases their chances of selecting a day when the bitch will have ovulated.

Ch. "PR" Hopkins' Fashionette, one of the fine females from Eliza Hopkins' kennel.

Don't assume that your bitch's interest in males will diminish after she has been bred. Continue to exercise caution in protecting her. Your bred bitch could still slip out under a fence. Males have been known to go to extraordinary lengths in their efforts to reach a female in season. You must remain vigilant.

During the final phase of your bitch's season, she will no longer be willing to stand for breeding. She may growl or snap at any male who attempts to mount her. Her swelling will diminish and her decreasing discharge will have changed to a dull brown color. Her body is now returning to normal.

As we have said, all TFT bitches are individuals. Some simply don't follow the commonly accepted rules. There are bitches that routinely have irregular seasons. They may be ready for breeding on the second day of their season. Conversely, one occasionally finds a bitch that should be bred on the sixteenth day. It is very difficult to ascertain the optimum breeding day for such females. You may breed this type of bitch, season after season, without getting her to conceive. You may want to coordinate with your veterinarian. He can perform vaginal smears that will help to pinpoint the ideal day for breeding.

DETERMINING PREGNANCY

The breeding has taken place and now the waiting game begins. If this will be your first litter, you will undoubtedly be anxious. You will be watching eagerly for any sign that your bitch is pregnant. I'm afraid there is nothing to do but relax. During the first month of pregnancy, there is virtually no way to tell for certain if your female has conceived.

The standard gestation period for dogs is 63 days. This is calculated from the date of the first breeding. I have found, however, that the majority of Toy Fox Terriers usually whelp before this date. Most of my females whelp about two full calendar months after their first breeding, or at 60 – 61 days. I have had a few rare bitches deliver their puppies at 56 days. On rare occasions, I have also had bitches who carried their puppies longer than 63 days. I make it a practice to watch my females very closely when they reach their eighth week.

Gr. Ch. "PR" Gorden's Madam Butterfly, owned by Doug and Betty Gorden, of Crosby, Texas.

A very pregnant "PR" Cody's Crystal, owned by W.D. and Dorothy Cody, of Tulsa, Oklahoma. The day after this photo was taken, Crystal gave birth to five pups.

You may be able to detect signs of pregnancy as early as the fourth week. At this stage, you might note a thickening in the width of the loin.

During the fifth week, other changes may become evident. Your bitch may become ravenous, eating her food with great relish. Bitches, particularly those carrying large litters, may look fuller in the belly. It is during the fifth week of pregnancy that you can palpate the bitch in an attempt to feel the developing fetuses. Some breeders are very skilled at palpation, while others just don't have the touch. The same applies to veterinarians. Palpation is effective only in the fifth week for at this stage the fetuses are small, hard and firm. Later, they will be too soft to detect. You should also know that if the bitch is carrying her puppies high up under the ribs, you won't be able to detect them. If you are going to palpate, above all, be gentle. You want to know if there are puppies. The last thing you want to do is harm them. With your thumb and index finger, gently feel along the bitch's abdomen. You are searching for one or more bumps approximately the size of a hickory nut. Once again, palpation is not foolproof. Don't become discouraged if you can't feel anything. We rely most on looking for a filling out in the flank, rather than palpation.

During the sixth week, you should be able to see definite signs of pregnancy. Your bitch may well have a big belly by the sixth week. Because of the added weight, her topline may begin to sag. Even bitches with strong, sound rears may appear spraddle-legged and cowhocked. You may see that the bitch's nipples are slightly swollen and appear more prominent. The breasts may begin to fill with milk. Remember, however, that your bitch could be carrying a single puppy, or be experiencing a false pregnancy. Do watch her closely even if you fear that she may not have conceived. Some breeders routinely have bitches x-rayed prior to the delivery. Your vet may note the size of the unborn puppies. It is comforting to have an idea of the approximate number of puppies so that you will know, to the greatest degree possible, when the birthing process is completed. Please be aware, however, that in litters with several puppies, there is often a puppy that is not detected on the x-ray.

CARING FOR THE MOTHER-TO-BE

Your bitch is now eating for herself and her puppies, and you will have to gauge her feedings appropriately. There are several theories on how best to feed a pregnant bitch. The goal is to provide adequate nourishment but not to allow the bitch to gain excess weight that will only make delivery more difficult. Consult with your vet regarding if and when to increase the pregnant bitch's feedings. Another factor to consider is the quality of her food. Foods high in protein, with a good calcium content, are recommended. Again, consult your vet to determine if you need to change your current feed. Two weeks after my females have been bred, I switch them to a high quality puppy food. I do not increase the amount of food during the first four weeks of pregnancy, in order to avoid an out-of-condition, flabby bitch that will have difficulty whelping. I gradually increase food over the next four weeks until the bitch is consuming twice the amount of food she would ordinarily consume, dividing the total amount into two daily feedings.

During the early stages of her pregnancy, your bitch can continue with her routine exercise. If she has good muscle tone, the whelping will easier. By the fourth week, however, it is best to cut down on any really strenuous exercise. Jumping should definitely be curtailed. If your TFT is a house dog, it is best to stop her from jumping on and of furniture at this time. As her bulk increases, she will be less agile and she could injure herself. As she becomes increasingly heavy, you will have to take added precautions. You may want to separate her from the other dogs and allow her to exercise alone. During the final week of pregnancy a female will not want to exercise much. She will likely go out to potty and then want back in her whelping pen.

Unless absolutely necessary, the bitch should receive no medications or shots during her pregnancy. Your veterinarian will have to approve the use of any prescription or over-the-counter treatments.

Toy Fox Terriers are, generally, healthy and hardy dogs. They usually experience few problems during their pregnancies. Your best bet for avoiding problems during pregnancy is to begin with a healthy bitch. By conditioning her carefully, insuring correct exercise and feeding her sensibly, you will have prepared her for her job as a mother. As the date she's due to whelp approaches, watch her closely. By being vigilant, you will be able to see both the physical and behavioral changes, and avoid any problems.

Gr. Ch. "PR" Berryhill's Lisa Jane Case bred by Nelda Shoemake and owned by Mary Case.

WHELPING

Delivering a litter of puppies is a natural process for your bitch. We've all heard the stories of bitches that whelped their litter, without assistance, under the porch of an old farmhouse. There's even the old timer's story of the Foxhound bitch. It seems that the pregnant bitch was part of a pack in hot pursuit of its quarry. During the chase, the bitch stopped, whelped a puppy and cleaned it off. Taking it in her mouth, she rejoined the other pack members, continued the chase and then came home to deliver the rest of her litter.

Natural though it may be, some dogs do need assistance in bringing their puppies into the world. Toy dogs may encounter more problems than larger breeds. It's advisable for you to be there, just in case there's a problem. Toy Fox Terriers are, in general, excellent mothers. Some do, however, need a little help in getting started.

If this is the first time you've attended a mother-to-be, it's natural that you'll be nervous. Just don't let your anxiety consume you. Some bitch owners have panicked at the last moment and rushed the bitch to the veterinarian so he could do the whelping. The place for the bitch who's beginning labor is at home, unless complications force a trip to the vet. She'll be more relaxed in familiar surroundings.

Your best bet for staying calm is to educate yourself. If you know what to anticipate, the whole experience will seem less frightening to you. By learning as much as possible

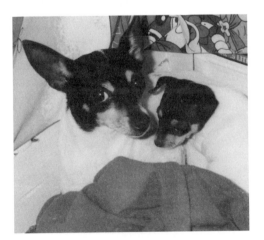

Lil' Miss Molly Kopischke and her puppy. Photo by Lorri Kopischke.

about what will happen, you'll be able to tell when things are going awry. It's impossible to predict how your bitch will act, particularly if this is her first litter. She may take command of the situation and not need any assistance at all. If she has the situation well in hand, don't interfere.

As the big day approaches, you're likely to become more and more anxious. Take heart, for most whelpings go smoothly, just as nature intended. To allay your fear, refer to this chapter and gather all the equipment that you might need. If you have a friend who's a long time breeder, keep the telephone close by. Many an experienced breeder has talked a novice through the process. If you truly fear that there might be a problem, check with your veterinarian. Tell him the date your bitch is due and make sure that he will be there or on call, should you need him during the night. If he does not take night calls, you will want to locate the nearest emergency all-night veterinary clinic.

WHERE TO HAVE THE PUPPIES

Left to her own devices, the bitch will surely choose an inappropriate place to whelp. Stories of bitches who delivered their litters in closets, in a dryer with the door left ajar, under the living room sofa, or in the middle of a bed, abound. Give some thought to where you want to house the mom and her litter. You want a place that's free from drafts and reasonably warm. Most importantly, you want a place where mom can feel secure and where she'll stay calm. Look for a spot that's away from the hustle and bustle of everyday life. You'll also want a location where you can easily glance in and check on her. If you have a guest bedroom, or there's a convenient corner of your bedroom, this may be ideal. It's possible that you'll have several nights when you'll be half awake, watching the bitch. Having access to a bed, for naps, is handy. If at all possible, you'll want a telephone within easy reach, just in case you do have an emergency.

Your bitch needs to feel protected and secure. This isn't the time to plan a dinner party or issue an invitation to the family to come for a visit. Keep strangers and friends alike away from the bitch. Don't bring people in to see the expectant mother. If there are children in your home, declare the mother-to-be's room strictly off limits. Expectant mothers have been known to act unpredictably.

It's best to provide the bitch with a whelping box. There are many types of boxes, some fancy and some simple, that may be used for the bitch. My whelping boxes are made of plywood or durable plastic and measure approximately 24 inches long, 15 inches wide and 18 inches high. Each breeder seems to come up with a design that suits him. There are, however, several guidelines you should follow. You must be able to sanitize the box. You'll want to make sure the mother has an opportunity to get

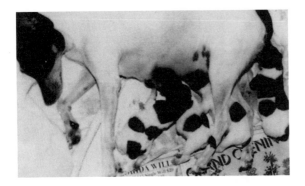

Kathleen Cornwell's Ch. "PR" Windy Acres' Tara nurses her litter of four.

away from the puppies. She must have easy access to them, but be able to escape their constant demands. The lip of the box must be low enough for the mother to easily get in and out but high enough to keep the newborns from rolling out of the box. I use soft fleece bedding or towels for bedding and change the bedding daily.

The whelping box is placed inside an eight-panel exercise pen. The pen is placed on a tarp and the floor is lined with newspapers. If the expectant bitch is kept in a kennel with other dogs, we suggest you enclose the bitch's pen so she can be isolated from the view of the other dogs.

It's best to place the mother in the whelping pen about a week to 10 days before she's due to whelp. This way she can become accustomed to her new surroundings. Mothers, suddenly placed in a new and strange whelping box, have been known to try relocating their litters to a place of their own choosing. Encourage her and tell her how good she is for remaining in this strange, new place. By the time she's ready to deliver the litter, she will have settled down and will be comfortable in her new home.

Most TFTs will be fine in your normal household temperature. Freedom from drafts, however, is essential. You don't want to take a chance on the puppies or the mother being chilled. You'll want to provide extra warmth during the whelping and for the first few days. We locate the whelping pen near the electric furnace in the kennel and elevate the temperature to 80 degrees for the first few days. If your bitch is whelping in your home you may wish to purchase a portable heater to heat the room in which she and the puppies are housed. I am leery of spot heating with heat lamps for fear they will overheat the area or create a fire hazard. When a puppy had to be hand raised, or separated from the mother for a period of time, I have used a heating pad on a low to medium setting and wrapped in a towel to prevent direct contact with the puppy.

WHAT ELSE WILL I NEED?

It's best to collect a few supplies that may come in handy during the whelping. Have a good supply of *newspapers* on hand and a large *garbage bag* for bundling up the soiled papers. It's a good idea to have a *small box* with a heat source, such as the heating pad described above. Some mothers become restless while they're whelping. You may want to remove one or more puppies and place them in this box, while she completes her delivery. You'll want to have a couple of *towels*, for cleaning and rubbing down the puppies. A pair of blunt nose *scissors* is excellent for use in cutting the umbilical cords. You might also prefer to have a *hemostat* on hand, for clamping the cord before you make the cut. Some breeders prefer to use *dental floss* to tie off the cords. It's best, just in case, to have some milk replacer or goat's milk on hand. You'll also want a *scale* (we find a food scale with a deep bowl an excellent choice) for weighing the newborns and a *pen* and *calendar* for recording the birth date and twice-daily weights.

HOW MANY PUPPIES CAN I EXPECT?

As far as I know, no one has ever taken a survey to determine the exact number of puppies contained in the average Toy Fox Terrier litter. From my experience (based on breeding bitches that conform, in size, to the standard), I would say that two to three puppy litters are the most common. I have had litters of five and know of others with six. Such numbers may be a mixed blessing. Puppies will need to be weighed and monitored carefully to make sure they are gaining weight, after the initial 24 hours when some weight loss is expected. If there is not subsequent weight gain, the breeder may need to supplement. The bitch's calcium level may need to be tested and if low, calcium supplementation is needed to prevent eclampsia. It is so much better to have a healthy litter of two or three than to deal with these problems that may result from a large litter. Don't be discouraged if your bitch doesn't appear to be pregnant. Litters of one are fairly common with Toy Fox Terriers.

Ch. "PR" Hopkins' Gay Tammy poses with her history making litter. This litter, which included Ch. "PR" Hopkins' Gay Danny and Ch. "PR" Hopkins' Gay Dottie, was the first born with a three generation, all champion pedigree. This record making litter was bred by Eliza Hopkins.

There's really no way that you can guess, in advance, how many puppies your bitch will produce. It is possible to have your bitch x-rayed to determine number of puppies, though occasionally a puppy will be hidden from view. You will, however, be able to get a fairly good idea when whelping has ended.

YOU AND YOUR VETERINARIAN

We hope that you've already established a close working relationship with your veterinarian. It's reassuring to know that you have someone you can trust, if need be. Don't pester your vet with calls over trivial, insignificant matters as the day of birth approaches. You don't want to gain a reputation as the boy who cried wolf. Make sure you keep records, such as the days your bitch was bred and the hour she went into labor. These will be helpful to your veterinarian, should treatment or intervention be necessary.

Let common sense be your guide in contacting your veterinarian for help. Some vets will tell you not to worry if the bitch hasn't gone into hard labor, meaning she has had at least one contraction. However, if you honestly believe there is a problem, do make a call. Trust your instincts. While your veterinarian is a well trained professional, you live with the bitch daily and know her better than anyone else. If you're sure there's a problem, don't hesitate to pick up the phone.

WATCHING FOR THE SIGNS

Toy Fox Terrier bitches vary in the warning they will give you as the time of birth approaches. Some exhibit virtually no symptoms. Conversely, other bitches will drive you to distraction several days before the big event. Many bitches

Judy Threlfall is "pretty sure" this little female is pregnant.

become excited, nervous and restless as the big day approaches. There are a few, however, who will remain calm until they go into labor. We have found when the mother-to-be refuses her treat of a dog biscuit that labor is not far off!

One of the early signs to look for is your bitch's attempt to 'nest' by arranging and rearranging her bedding. She may appear agitated, tearing at the bedding and scratching around in the bedding. Many bitches refuse food as the time approaches. Some wolf down their food voraciously, only to regurgitate it afterward. You may notice that your bitch is shivering violently, even though the temperature in the room is very warm. Sometimes you can detect a physical change in your bitch's appearance. She may be carrying her puppies lower and have a hollow look in the loin area.

Some bitches, particularly household pets, want you near them at this time. Give your TFT a few pats of encouragement, try to calm her down and tell her how well she's doing. Stay calm your self. This period, know as pre-labor, may last only an hour or last the better part of a day.

TEMPERATURE AS AN INDICATOR

Most breeders will rely on their experience in determining when a bitch is due to whelp. For the beginner, however, charting your bitch's temperature can be helpful. The bitch's temperature will drop shortly before the birth of the puppies. By taking her temperature twice a day, you'll have advance warning.

The dog's normal temperature is around 101.6 degrees. Individual dogs can vary slightly from the accepted norm. For this reason, it is best to take your bitch's temperature twice a day during the week before she is due to whelp, to determine her norm. Take your readings at 12-hour intervals, such as 7:00 a.m. and 7:00 p.m. Avoid taking the reading immediately after your bitch has exercised, as activity may elevate the temperature. Don't be alarmed if her temperature fluctuates slightly during the day. This is normal.

When you notice a steep drop in the bitch's temperature, you'll want to watch her closely. The temperature will probably drop into the nineties. This is a clear sign that your bitch will whelp some time within the next 24 hours. If you see no symptoms of labor within a day after the temperature drops, phone your veterinarian. Similarly, if your bitch has not whelped by the 63rd day after breeding, it's best to take her in for a check-up.

LABOR BEGINS

During the first stage of labor, your bitch will become increasingly nervous and uncomfortable. She'll scratch frantically at her bedding, lie down, and pant for a few seconds and then get up to paw again. She may have a pained look on her face. Don't be alarmed if she whines and trembles. Watch for your bitch to begin licking her vulva. You don't want to interfere with her at this stage. It's best to keep an eye on her from a discreet distance. Don't add to her nervousness.

The beginning stage of labor may last one hour or more. You might try speeding up the process by letting the bitch outside to relieve herself. Offer her a drink of water. Do exercise caution and keep a close eye on her while she's outside. More than one breeder has discovered that the bitch whelped a puppy while outside.

If your bitch remains in this first stage of labor for more than 24 hours, call your veterinarian. Problems don't usually occur until the bitch has gone into hard labor, but it is best to be on the safe side. Do keep an eye out for an abnormal discharge. If you see a greenish or black discharge, phone the vet immediately. Excessive bleeding should also be reported promptly to your veterinarian. You have worked too hard up to this point to not take every action to insure that every puppy is born alive and well. No inconvenience and expense is worth losing a puppy.

HARD LABOR

Hard labor begins when your bitch has her first contraction. The first contractions could be mild and easily missed, so watch closely. You don't want to interfere, but it's best, at this stage, to move closer and keep a steady eye on her. Jot down the time you noticed the first contraction. Don't trust your memory. The contractions will probably increase as your bitch bears down. The contractions may follow one right after the other or there may be an interval of time between them. Much of this depends on where the puppies are, in relation to the birth canal. If this is the first time you've witnessed a bitch in labor, it may look as though she's straining to have a bowel movement. Your bitch will choose a position that's comfortable for her. Some bitches have their puppies lying down and some prefer to stand.

If your bitch is having very hard contractions and she hasn't whelped a puppy in an hour, it is time to call the veterinarian. There may be an overly large puppy that she's unable to expel. It is also possible that a puppy is in an awkward position and jammed at the entrance to the birth canal. In either of these situations, your vet may elect to perform a Caesarian section. If your bitch's hard contractions stop suddenly and don't resume within an hour, call the vet.

THEY'RE HERE!

After one or several hard contractions, a large, black, bubble-like sac will emerge from the vulva. This will probably be the water bag. The appearance of the water bag is an important sign, for it signals the entrance of the first puppy into the birth canal. Be alert, for the puppy usually follows quickly. Occasionally, the water bag will burst in the birth canal, but this is not a cause for alarm.

Most puppies are born headfirst. The puppy will be encased in a watertight, fluid filled sac. During the months of pregnancy, he has been suspended in this fluid and received oxygen through his umbilical cord. The sac must be torn away from the puppy's head immediately, so that he can breathe air, not fluid, now that the umbilical cord is no longer providing him with oxygen. Make sure the bitch attends to this immediately. If she does not, tear the sac away with your fingers. Move quickly. Try to be unobtrusive, so as to avoid upsetting the bitch unnecessarily.

Generally, the bitch will take over. She'll pull away and eat the sac. She'll lick the puppy all over, cleaning it and stimulating it. You will be surprised at how roughly the bitch handles the newborn. She may even roll the puppy over, causing it to cry out and thrash around. Don't be alarmed. This is natural and beneficial. As the pup cries out, he's filling his newborn lungs with oxygen.

On most occasions, when the bitch has finished cleaning the puppy, she should attend to the umbilical cord. She will sever it with her teeth. Occasionally the puppy will be still attached by the umbilical cord to the unexpelled placenta. You may take a soft wash cloth and pull on the cord gently. If the placenta does not appear, you may wish to clamp the cord then cut the cord. Some inexperienced mothers neglect to cut the cord. Take a firm hold on the cord, but do not pull it as this will result in an umbilical hernia. Approximately one to two inches from the puppy's belly is where you want to cut the cord. Some breeders prefer to clamp the cord first with a hemostat. If you opt for this method, leave the clamp in place for a few minutes or until the bleeding subsides. Some breeders also feel it is best to tie the cord. If you want to tie the cord, encircle it with dental floss and make one or two knots. Be sure to cut off all the excess floss. If you don't trim the floss, it will worry the mother and she may tug on it and injure the puppy.

Be sure to look for the placenta, or afterbirth. This is usually attached to the umbilical cord. The afterbirth is about half the size of the puppy and will resemble a dark piece of liver. Occasionally, the placenta will separate from the puppy and be expelled just after he's born or be pushed out by the emergence of the next puppy.

"PR" Casas Adobe's Amber, owned by Judy Guillot, of Tucson, Arizona, at one day of age. Photo by David Ring.

I'm here and I'm bored already. Judy Threlfall's babies.

You'll want to be alert for the appearance of each afterbirth. There will be one for every puppy born. You may want to make a note each time you see one. After the whelping is completed, check your notes. If an afterbirth was not expelled, contact your veterinarian. Retained placentas cause very serious infections and may be fatal to your bitch.

Breeders differ in their opinions as to whether the mother should be allowed to eat the afterbirths. The afterbirth is a rich source of vitamins and nutrients. In the wild, it supplies the mother with nourishment so that she doesn't have to leave the litter in search of food. Experts also believe that the placenta may stimulate milk production. Unfortunately, consuming the afterbirth has a laxative effect on the bitch and she's apt to have loose stools for a few days. Some breeders remove and discard all afterbirths. Many breeders allow the bitch to eat one afterbirth and remove all subsequent ones. Other breeders believe it is best to allow the bitch to consume as many as she wants. We fall into this last group. Talk with your vet, or friends who are experienced breeders, to help you decide what to do.

CLEARING THE PUPPY OF FLUID

Once the mother has cleaned up the puppy, you'll want to pick him up and examine him. Some mothers object to this, while others seem to welcome the help. If the mother objects and you feel she's done a good job, you can delay your examination. Once you proceed with your examination, rub the puppy vigorously with a towel until he's completely dried. Remember, you needn't be gentle. If he hasn't made a sound or if he seems a little sluggish, give a sharp little tug on his tail. This is akin to spanking a newborn human infant and he'll cry out and his lungs will fill with oxygen. I have rubbed a puppy born blue and oxygen deprived for 45 minutes until it pinked up.

Hold the puppy to your ear. If you hear any rasping, rattling or bubbling, the puppy has retained fluid in its lungs. You don't want him to get pneumonia, so it's best to deal with this immediately. You'll want to swing down or shake down the puppy, as breeders call this technique. While it may sound complicated, once you try it you will see how simple it is in reality. Hold the puppy very securely, with his belly resting in your palm. Place the other hand over its back, with the index finger and middle finger behind the puppy's neck and head for support. Stand up straight with your legs approximately shoulder's width apart. Carefully raise the puppy, at arm's length, over your head. Make sure your grip is secure so you do not drop him. Swing your arms forcefully in an arc, from over your head to down between your legs. The centrifugal force generated in this maneuver will expel fluid from the puppy's lungs. You'll notice a few bubbles of moisture at the puppy's nose and or mouth. Wipe these off and repeat the procedure. Place the puppy to your ear once again. If you still hear rasping, repeat the procedure. Continue with this until the puppy's lungs sound clear.

After whelping, the new mother will attend to her puppies, nursing and licking them. She will likely doze herself, exhausted from the birth process. She will need to eat, but may be nervous about leaving her brood. One puppy squeak and she will tear back to the nesting box. She may or may not take the time to eat her normal ration. Since you will want her to eat as much as she desires, you may have to tempt her. We routinely mix cottage cheese, canned dog food, and softened puppy food and heat it to take the chill off and to make the aroma irresistible. The cottage cheese adds calcium to the lactating bitch's diet. Consult your vet about supplementing with calcium and/or monitoring the bitch's calcium level with a blood test. You may have to place the bowl in the box if she won't leave her puppies. We have had to resort to hand feeding this warmed 'stew' to a particularly hypervigilant mother. A small amount of puppy replacer milk can be added to further tempt the mother. Breeders often have a supply of baby food strained meat jars on hand to tease back the taste buds of a new mom. I have found that heating strained baby chicken and allowing the mother to lick it off my fingers will engage the most nervous mother in eating. Obviously, fresh water and dry kibble should be accessible at all times.

THE FAMILY GROWS

Bitches may deliver their puppies in rapid succession, or there could be a lengthy break before the next puppy

What could be more charming than a TFT puppy? Robbie Overstreet, of Richmound, Texas, holds 8 week old Thomas Jefferson in the palm of her hand. He weighs a single pound.

arrives. It will calm the bitch if you leave the puppy with her, until the next contractions begin. Many bitches become restless when the contractions start again. They stand, walk around and tear at the bedding. It is best to remove the first puppy, so that mom can concentrate on the task at hand. You would not want her to lie on the pup or inadvertently injure him. Be sure to place him on a heating pad that has been wrapped in a towel.

It is entirely possible that the second puppy may come breech or feet first. Such births are fairly common in dogs. Breech puppies may come easily. There is the possibility, however, that the puppy may hang up since the widest part of his body, the shoulders, exits last. Some bitches must give an extra push or two to expel the pup. If the hind legs emerge, but the rest of the pup does not immediately follow, you should help complete the birth process. Grasp the hind legs with a terry cloth wash cloth and hold them securely. If at all possible, leave the sac intact. Pull gently, steadily and very slowly. It is best to pull in time with the mother's contractions. If she isn't bearing down, massage her stomach to stimulate the contractions. Make certain you pull out and down, just as the puppy would come into the world naturally. Once the puppy is out, quickly break the sac, clean and massage the puppy, and swing him down. This is very important, as breech puppies almost always have fluid in their lungs.

Experienced breeders can often successfully turn a puppy, which is in an abnormal position inside the mother. They have learned this skill from watching veterinarians, talking with breeders, and through experience. It is difficult for novices to deal with this type of problem, however. A call to your veterinarian is in order.

HELPING THE PUPPIES TO NURSE

Now that the puppies are here, it's time for them to nurse. Some puppies instinctively hunt for a nipple almost immediately while others may not nurse for an hour or more. First time mothers may be uncomfortable having the puppies nurse. Don't worry. With time and patience the bitch will catch on.

The first feeding is very important. Following birth, the mother produces colostrum. This milky substance contains antibodies that transfer the mother's immunities to the puppies. If a puppy seems reluctant to nurse, you will have to lend a helping hand. Open the puppy's mouth by putting pressure on both corners of the mouth and forcing the jaws open and then place the open mouth on a nipple. Squeeze a few drops of milk onto the puppy's tongue. If necessary, support his body while he nurses. Getting a newborn to nurse is sometimes frustrating, but just keep at it. Soon you'll be rewarded by a row of contented little puppies with full tummies.

THE CAESARIAN BITCH

We hope that your bitch won't need a Caesarian section, but just in case, there are a few special tips for handling a C-section bitch and her family. Much of the success of the Caesarian will depend upon your veterinarian. There is no denying that some veterinarians are more skilled than others in performing this operation. Techniques vary. Some vets make a small incision, while others make a very large cut. It is absolutely essential that your veterinarian be well schooled in administering anesthesia to toy dogs. Sad to say, some bitches have been overdosed and failed to regain consciousness.

The veterinarian will probably have an assistant to help him during the operation. If he can't contact someone on short notice, you may have to assist. The vet will handle the bitch and you'll see to the puppies. Dry them off and swing them, if necessary, just as you would in a natural birth.

It is difficult to predict how quickly your bitch will regain consciousness. Much depends on how much anesthesia the veterinarian has used. Discuss this with the vet. Ask him how long you can expect the bitch to be affected and call him back if she hasn't roused in that time. Keep the bitch warm until she comes completely out from the effects of the anesthesia.

Caesarian mothers sometimes have trouble accepting their puppies. Bitches who have already had a litter will usually adapt more readily to the situation. They have had puppies before and will usually respond to their natural mothering instincts. If this is your bitch's first litter things could be a bit tricky. Remember, she has just come through a very stressful situation. She remembers being in pain. She was then whisked away to a strange place with unusual smells, someone gave her a shot and she remembers nothing else. If this is her first litter, she has never seen newborn puppies before. They are strange little things and they have been placed in her pen, which is her territory. Chances are the puppies are crying or making sounds that are new to her. Under these conditions, the bitch may move aggressively on the puppies or ignore them. In both instances, you must remain with the litter to intervene appropriately. Get the puppies as close to mom as you can. The sooner they start to smell like her, the sooner she'll accept them. With the indifferent mother, we have had success in bonding pups to mom by holding their bottoms up to her mouth to lick. This triggers the natural mothering instincts.

Caesarian puppies will have absorbed some of the anesthesia. They may be a little more sluggish than vaginally born puppies. You may have to work longer to get them to successfully nurse. To make matters more complicated, the mother is apt to be sore and may be reluctant to have them nurse. Gradually the bitch will accept her new charges. You may have to briefly provide some supplemental formula for a few feedings if the process is prolonged, but be persistent in your efforts to have the mother assume responsibility for her litter.

SUPPLEMENTING WEAK PUPPIES

Inevitably you will encounter puppies that for some reason will not or cannot nurse regularly. Oftentimes these are tiny puppies, but not always so. One recent 2 1/2-oz. newborn started nursing soon after birth and became the heaviest in the litter, weighing 37 oz. at 8 weeks. A heavier 4-oz puppy in the same litter lost weight and had to be hand fed until weaning. This puppy weighed 26 oz. at 8 weeks. In other words, just when one thinks there might be some logic involved, you discover there isn't.

Regardless of the correctness of your intervention, some puppies will not be saved. Yet we try valiantly to sustain the tiny life and grieve when our efforts are unsuccessful. We are somewhat comforted by the fact that our veterinarians and we have done everything possible and that internal medical problems beyond our control were probably in operation in such a case.

The case for charting the weight of ALL puppies in a litter at least twice per day cannot be emphasized enough. If you wait until you notice physical signs of malnourishment, it may be too late. Nothing can replace armchair patrol at the whelping box to note which pups are able to nurse and which aren't. The tendency is to want to put these puppies on a teat until they are full, but some pups come off the teat when the mother moves, lick it or other pups push it away. The mothers are also nervous about this intervention. I have virtually pried a puppy's mouth open and placed it on a teat only to have it immediately come off the teat. This is an ominous sign that hand rearing may be the only solution.

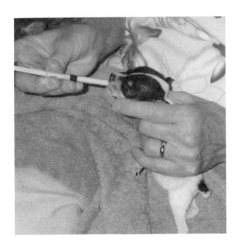

We have used the commercially prepared artificial bitch's milk or canned goat's milk with success. Most veterinarians and pet shops stock such milk and as delivery approaches you should have a can on hand. I also found both late one night stocked at our 24 hour super store. We also administer a baby pea sized helping of

Sally Davidson feeds 2 oz Sammy with a 1cc TB syringe.

Nutrical prior to feeding the milk. Calories and the resultant energy are integral at this important time.

We have tried several methods of delivering the milk to the pups –all with limited success. It is extremely difficult to regulate the amount of milk that a puppy can swallow with most of these methods. Pneumonia from aspirated milk becomes the problem and the pup dies slowly unless an antibiotic can thwart the infection. The drops from an eyedropper are not consistent in size and one large drop can overpower a tiny throat. The holes on the nipples on nursing bottles are difficult to regulate. We have used minuscule stomach feeding tubes, but have too often ended up with milk exiting the nose, because we have over filled the stomach.

The only method that has worked at Meadowood is the use of a 1 cc. tuberculin syringe (needle removed, of course). The one cc is equivalent to one fifth of a teaspoon. With her nursing background, Sally believed this would be the best way to deliver small amounts of milk while minimizing the possibility of aspiration. Practice in the sink releasing one drop at a time. There are about 5 drops in a tenth of a cc. Point the syringe toward the inner cheek (again to reduce the chance of aspiration) and watch for the puppy to swallow. Wait a few seconds and then release another drop. When the puppy is slow to swallow, discontinue feeding. You may have fed as little as .2 of a cc, but it all got to its destination without creating other problems. In 2 hours you will try again and continue around the clock. We do heat in the microwave (6 seconds at high) about a teaspoon of the milk in a teacup until warm (not hot) and test on the inner wrist before administering.

Eventually pups start to suck on the end of the syringe as you slowly release their milk. You may lay the pup on your lap and lightly drum their back with two fingers to expel air and burp the puppy. They will burp within a minute if they need to.

When returning the pups to the mother, encourage the mother to lick the urethra and anus to encourage elimination. If the pup is orphaned, a cotton ball moistened with warm water should be used to massage the urethra and anus to produce elimination.

Puppies that fail to thrive may have to be taken from the dam for constant care. We believe in giving every puppy the nourishment and environment that will allow it to survive.

A newborn does not develop a shivering response until the sixth day. This response allows him to stabilize internal heat. Nonetheless, it will be the third or fourth week before a puppy can independently maintain a normal body temperature of 101 degrees. Normal puppies depend upon the dam to supply warmth, but the weak pup may not be able to nest next to the dam. Chilled puppies will not nurse, so body temperature needs to be raised first. Every breeder has her or his own ideas on the best way to incubate puppies. We do not use heat lamps because of the risk

Two oz Sammy grew to be a full sized TFT. Pictured with new owners Alex and Dan Kinstedt.

of fire, fear that the light could fall, and the inability of weak pups to move away from hot spots. Dehydration under a heat lamp can occur very quickly. Heating pads can also heat erratically and are often kept too hot for the puppy.

There are rheostat-controlled rubberized mats available from pet supply catalogs that are ideal for maintaining a constant, safe temperature. Short of that, we have had success with a dependable heating pad set on low, wrapped in a thick towel. This towel-wrapped pad is then put in a small box and placed in a room that is 80 degrees (often a small bathroom with the door kept shut). Please note that we do not feel comfortable recommending this method, as we do not know your heating pad. We sleep only a few feet from our orphans and constantly check the towel's warmth. We feel this level of vigilance allows us to use the pad with success.

As mentioned previously, we chart how much milk is ingested and the puppy's weight prior to feeding. Any gain is seen as a success. There will be periods of time with small losses or no gain at all. We are more concerned about sustaining life at this point until the pup is sufficiently strong to nurse vigorously.

We feed every two hours around the clock during the first week. This may be extended to three hours the second week if the pup is gaining. One can go to four-hour intervals when the puppy doubles his birth weight.

TAIL DOCKING AND DEWCLAW REMOVAL

Although veteran breeders may handle these tasks themselves, it is obviously NOT a task for a novice. It was twenty-five years into breeding TFTs before I felt comfortable enough to attempt tail docking and dew claw removal. Even then, it was after careful tutelage by my own veterinarian and several mentors in the breed. I would advise that you make an appointment to take your puppies on the third day to your veterinarian. We have occasionally waited an extra day to dock puppies that are extremely small and/or weak.

Removal of dewclaws has both practical and aesthetic considerations. If you have ever tried to cut dewclaws on a struggling dog you know how difficult it can be to do so. Another practical concern is that dewclaws can become easily caught or snagged and leave your TFT open to injury. As to appearances, your TFT will benefit from a cleaner look to the leg as a result of removal.

This is a simple procedure and may produce a quick cry from the pup as if it is being pinched. We use a small fingernail scissors, reserved for this task only, and sterilized with alcohol prior to use. My wife holds the puppy under good light and I gently pull the dewclaw away from the leg. This will create a small mound of skin and nail which is snipped directly behind this mound. A moistened styptic powder is applied with a little pressure via a cotton swab. Although dewclaws are routinely found on the front legs, one will occasionally appear on hind legs also. Always check! I found my first set of hind dewclaws recently after 35 years in the breed.

The importance of the tail to the total image of the TFT has already been discussed under the chapter on the standard. Unfortunately, not all veterinarians are familiar with the breed and the appropriate length of the tail. Because the length of tail is so important, you may ask to be consulted before each snip of the surgeon's tool.

The UKC standard requires that a full 3/5 of the puppies tail be removed while the AKC standard advocates for removal at the third or fourth joint. We have not found using a ruler to measure the tail very effective, as puppy tails can vary widely in length. Taking off a strictly measured 3/5 of the tail may leave some tails too long and others short. Our method has managed to produce tails of correct length for both registries.

Our method involves sliding the thumb and forefinger down the length of the undocked puppy's tail, starting at the base. You'll see and feel that the tail is broader at the base, where it joins the body. You'll also note that a very short way down, the tail begins to taper. Look and feel for this point. The cut should always be made where the taper begins. We mark that point with a fine, felt tip marker and both of us check the tail again to be sure.

We use a guillotine nail cutter, used solely for this procedure, which is sterilized with alcohol prior to each use. The tail is sufficiently pinched so that bleeding is reduced and we apply a styptic mixture to tail and apply pressure. Some veterinarians like to put a stitch at the end of the tail, but we have not noted any particular advantage in doing so.

We do these procedures in the house well away from the puppies' dam. She would be unduly disturbed by the procedures. We check each puppy to be sure that all bleeding has stopped and take them back to their dam. She will examine them carefully and the puppies will be nursing in no time. We check the puppies frequently the rest of that day to insure their recovery. Occasionally a bitch may lick the puppies vigorously and open a wound, but this does not happen often.

We have not dealt with the issue of docking naturally bobbed puppy tails. Oh, if they could only be born with the right length tail! If the tail is already too short or just a nub, the decision is made for you. However, the tail may be only 3/4 of an inch in length and still have to be docked. Again use the taper method to locate the appropriate docking point. After marking the tail, I try as best I can to stack the puppy and hiding the part of the tail that will be removed, I hold the tail up to see if it is in proportion at this point.

I once purchased a natural bobbed bitch whose tail should have been docked. At that time, we could show 3-6 month old puppies and I was consistently told that the tail was too long. My veterinarian said that he could dock the tail, but at this age it involved anesthesia and surgery. My experience was not positive. The tail took a long time to heal and regrow hair and the bitch had to wear an Elizabethan collar to prevent her from licking the tail and opening the wound. The bitch did finish quickly and became a great brood matron, but personally I decided I would never go through that again.

We do not believe that these two minor procedures cause much more than a pinch of pain to the whelps. At three days, the puppy's circulatory and nervous systems are not fully developed and the puppy's bones are still soft. We believe that whatever outcry we hear from the puppies is as much from the strangeness of the procedure as from actual pain.

In today's environment, the docking of tails has become increasingly under fire in some countries and outright illegal in others. In Australia, TFTs are called Mini Foxies and tails may not be docked. Some breeders are experimenting with producing a line of naturally bobbed puppies. As discussed previously, the length of the natural bob can vary widely and there is always the chance of whelping a puppy with no tail. Another concern is whether such a line might be more prone to spinabifida- research is incomplete at his time.

The fancy may just have to adjust to undocked specimens in the future. Whereas the dewclaw removal can be a health issue, the TFT was originally docked so that it would look like the Smooth Fox Terrier. The Smooth Fox Terriers tail is docked longer and served as a handle to extricate the terrier from underground . However, if as much of the TFT tail was left on as the Smooth, this TFT tail might sweep back over the back rather than stay straight and erect as the longer Smooth's tail. An undocked TFT tail would likely mimic that of the Chihuahua in style and in proportional length.

THE DAM'S HEALTH

It is not unusual for the bitch to show some discharge for 2 or 3 days after whelping. If it continues beyond that or if the discharge becomes black or green, you will need to have the bitch checked for possible infection. My vet likes to give a shot of pitocin soon after whelping to clamp down the uterus and expel any foreign material that might be left behind.

Allow the dam to eat all she can eat during lactation. She will likely double her usual ration. If not, we will spare no expense in finding some item high in calcium and/or protein that will tease her into eating. Human baby foods (meats) or high-grade canned dog food will often do the trick. Heating food also seems to bring out enticing aromas.

We have had to feed first time whelpers out of our hands, as they were loath to leave their babies to eat. Whatever happens, your task is to arouse a voracious appetite in the bitch, so that ample milk is supplied.

If a female is lactating heavily or has 4 or more puppies, you will want to watch for signs of calcium insufficiency. Excessive panting, repetitive scratching at bedding, involuntary nodding of the head and staggering behavior all are clues that the bitch needs a rapid infusion of calcium. Your vet may wish to introduce calcium via an IV or injection, as there may not be time enough to feed calcium-enriched food. We routinely feed cottage cheese to lactating bitches to increase the intake of calcium.

It cannot be stressed enough how important the dam's health and eating habits are tied to the success of her whelps. I will alter schedules and foods to get the lactating bitch eating again. The only alternative is hand rearing puppies, a difficult and time-consuming process.

THE PUPPIES GROW

The puppies' eyes will open at about two weeks of age. It's fascinating to watch them discover their new world. By two or three weeks, they'll be staggering onto their feet and trying to take their first faltering steps. In another

Puppies at play. Owned by Marsha Shively.

short week, they'll be walking without difficulty. However, if you've had a litter with only one puppy, it may take him a little longer to begin walking. You'll want to clip back the puppies' toenails at this stage. The tips can be taken off with a pair of fingernail scissors or a human nail clipper. Be careful to remove only the white tip and avoid cutting into the pink vein, known as the quick.

Puppy Ears

In the standard chapter, we discussed the variability of puppies' ears achieving permanent prick ear status. Generally the smaller puppy's ears will go up first and

the largest last. This does not mean that they will stay up permanently, as they are likely to go up and down daily, especially as the puppies teethe. Breeders have selectively bred to produce puppies whose ears will eventually be up right. Don't panic if your puppy's ears flop the morning after coming to your home. It is likely that the stress of changing residences and routines will precipitate such a problem, but they will rise again.

PUPPY HEALTH

Tuffy's ears on their way up. Owned by the Van Allens of Hudson, WI.

When puppies are weaned from their mother, it will be necessary to inoculate them for canine disease. The protection of immunity to disease, which comes from the mother's colostrum, will wane as the puppies are weaned. Consult your veterinarian about the timing and sequence of shots that will be used on the puppies.

You also may wish to have a fecal exam on a puppy's stool. Chances are that whatever one would have, they all would have. If parasites are present, your vet is your best resource in diagnosing and treating the problem. His medications are far more effective than most over-the-counter remedies.

When pups begin waddling around the box, a small pen can be erected, so they can start coming out of their bed to eliminate. At that time, you may blend water-softened puppy kibble with the canned bitch's milk, making a liquid gruel. We warm it and put it on a shallow cottage cheese lid. The puppies will walk

Making the transitions from mama to "real" food is this litter owned by Eliza Hopkins.

through it at the outset, but later will begin to lap it up. We offer this liquefied food 5 – 6 times per day, along with a continuous supply of dry kibble. The mother needs to be put in a separate pen during these feedings. At this stage we also allow continuous access to a small dish of water, tightly secured to the side of the pen. After a week or two, we mash water-softened food into a more solid state, warm and serve. Puppies are provided as much as they will eat. You will be surprised one day to hear crunching and realize the little ones are eating dry food! You know then that your puppies are on their way to continuous self-regulated eating of hard kibble only.

A lovely litter of TFTs. Owned by Julie and Al Slauterbeck.

SOCIALIZING PUPPIES

An acquaintance purchased a puppy at a pet shop and brought it home. He had a large fenced yard, but the puppy would not get off the sidewalk. The pup was afraid of the grass. Now it was perfectly comfortable on concrete and proceeded to relieve herself on the walk. It took a lot of patience to teach the puppy that grass was OK. The puppy had undoubtedly been raised in a kennel environment on concrete. An excellent TFT show dog was always nervous while being examined by male judges. His breeder and owner were single women who had not socialized the puppy to males. He would win consistently under female judges, but fold under men. Both of these examples illustrate the importance of socialization for all puppies regardless of their owner's goals.

One of the most important steps a breeder can take is to properly socialize puppies. The puppies may be beautiful and may meet their breed standard perfectly, but if their personality is tainted in anyway, they will never completely satisfy their owner. Puppies have to be exposed to different surfaces, sounds, environments and people. Their confidence has to be built up over time. Responsible breeders who have a kennel will likely understand this need while the back yard breeder's home-raised puppies may not necessarily be socialized. Raising them in the home does not automatically

Puppy meets Duck Kopischke's Lil' Darlin Daphne. Photo by Lorri Kopischke.

These pups, bred by John Davidson, of Dunlap, Illinois, are beginning to explore the world.

guarantee socialization, especially if the only person the pups see is the breeder. Margaret Hughes of Positive Paws Dog Training has created a system for socialization entitled *The Puppy's Rule of Twelve*. She has given permission to print this system at the end of this section.

We like to bring puppies in our home as they start to exert some independence of their dam. We want to build their confidence so that they are well adjusted in many social situations. We have had dinner parties where the entertainment for the evening was playing with our puppies. If there aren't many people coming through your home you might have to take the puppies to the people. We have literally called family and friends, so that we can go visit with puppies. Letting them be petted and/or accept a tiny treat leads the puppies to believe that strangers are OK. There may be a reticent pup in the litter. These are the ones that need special attention. Give them lots of one on one time and put them in your coat pocket and take them with you everywhere. Slowly, this puppy will come out of his shell and warm to social situations. You, of course, will bond with this puppy and tear up when it leaves for its new home!

As soon as the requisite shots are completed, enroll the pup in basic puppy obedience classes- again teaching that strange people as well as strange dogs are OK. An increasing number of pet stores encourage dogs to visit. Take advantage of this different environment by initially carrying your TFT through the store. I am always watchful for the larger dog that might be aggressive to toy dogs visiting the store. Walks, especially where the pup will encounter other folks, are very beneficial, but be aware everyone will want to pick up your TFT- beat them to it by holding him for them to pet. I have noted attendees at large outdoor events carrying very small puppies, with everyone stopping them to make over the little one. I am not sure that that much stimulation does much good and may be more about the proud parent's pride in their puppy than socialization. The hot, tired puppy looks as though he would be far more comfortable in his bed at home. I think more can be accomplished by several short trips out into the world.

Put the crate in the car occasionally and take a short trip to a park or somewhere fun. Don't let your dog's only car association be a trip to the vet. Our dogs

Puppies must get used to the other dogs.

love to travel in the car so much that they will jump in the car when we start to pack for a trip and refuse to come out.

Socialization is a time consuming, but necessary, part of the process of breeding dogs. However, it is the part that garners the most favor from puppy purchasers and attracts attention to your breed. People are attracted to a breed by its looks, but treasure the breed for its personality.

THE PUPPY'S RULE OF TWELVE

Positive Paws Dog Training 2002 – Margaret Hughes
Adapted with permission from Pat Schoop's Rule of 7's

Make sure all experiences are safe and positive for the puppy. Each encounter should include treats and lots of praise. Slow down and add distance if your puppy is scared! By the time a puppy is 12 weeks old (if your puppy is over 12 weeks start right away with this socialization guide), it should have:

Experienced 12 different surfaces: wood, wood chips, carpet, tile, cement, linoleum, grass, wet grass, dirt, mud, puddles, deep pea gravel, grates, uneven surfaces, on a table, on a chair, etc....

Played with 12 different objects: fuzzy toys, big and small balls, hard toys, funny sounding toys, wooden items, paper or cardboard items, milk jugs, metal items, car keys, etc....

Experienced 12 different locations: front yard (daily), other people's homes, school yard, lake, pond, river, boat, basement, elevator, car, moving car, garage, laundry room, kennel, veterinarian hospital (just to say "hi" & visit, lots of cookies, no vaccinations), grooming salon (just to say "hi"), etc....

Met and played with 12 new people (outside the family): include children, adults (mostly men), elderly adults, people in wheelchairs, walkers, people with canes, crutches, hats, sunglasses, etc....

Exposed to 12 different noises (ALWAYS keep positive and watch puppy's comfort level – we don't want the puppy scared): garage door opening, doorbell, children playing, babies screaming, big trucks, Harley motorcycles, skateboards, washing machine, shopping carts rolling, power boat, clapping, loud singing, pan dropping, horses neighing, vacuums, lawnmowers, birthday party, etc….

Exposed to 12 fast moving objects (don't allow to chase): skateboards, roller-skates, bicycles, motorcycles, cars, people running, cats running, scooters, vacuums, children running, children playing soccer, squirrels, cats, horses running, cows running, etc….

Experiences 12 different challenges: climb on, in, off and around a box, go through a cardboard tunnel, climb up and down steps, climb over obstacles, play hide & seek, go in and out a doorway with a step up or down, exposed to an electric sliding door, umbrella, balloons, walk on a wobbly table (plank of wood with a small rock underneath), jump over a broom, climb over a log, bathtub (and bath) etc….

Handled by owner (& family) 12 times a week: hold under arm (like a football), hold to chest, hold on floor near owner, hold in-between owner's legs, hold head, look in ears, mouth, in-between toes, hold and take temperature (ask veterinarian), hold like a baby, trim toe nails, hold in lap, etc….

Eaten from 12 different shaped containers: wobbly bowl, metal, cardboard box, paper, coffee cup, china, pie plate, plastic, frying pan, Kong, Treatball, Bustercube, spoon fed, paper bag, etc….

Eaten in 12 different locations: back yard, front yard, crate, kitchen, basement, laundry room, bathroom, friend's house, car, school yard, bathtub, up high (on work bench), under umbrella, etc….

Played with 12 different puppies (or safe adult dogs) as much as possible.
Left alone safely, away from family & other animals (5 – 45 minutes) 12 times a week.
Experienced a leash and collar 12 different times in 12 different locations.

TRAINING
THE SHOW PUPPY

If you hope to show your puppy, reread the section on socialization and magnify its importance times one hundred. Whether shown in AKC or UKC the Toy Fox Terrier must exert a proud, self-assured terrier type personality. Without all the work that goes into socialization, your show puppy will be at a disadvantage in the show ring. You can train the puppy to trot around the ring and to stand for examination, but unless those ears are up top, the tail at attention and the gait jauntily self-assured, he will not display the temperament of the Toy Fox Terrier. Every breeder has had a superior specimen of the breed that despite his/her best efforts did not show itself off in the ring. This is a breed where that is so important and even lesser specimens may win because they have that sparkly personality.

I have shown a very few Toy Fox Terriers over the years that were naturals. With very little training or ring experience I was occasionally able to put a lead on a dog that loved the ring and virtually barked " Look at me!" Recently I gave a best of sex win to an exhibitor who announced that it was the first time the dog had had a lead on! Believe me when I say this is the exception!

How would you feel if you arrived for work one morning and your boss asked you to give a speech to a group of strangers? Chances are great that you would be highly anxious. Yet this is what we too often expect out of six-month-old puppies. You put a lead on him and ran him down the driveway a couple of times and considered him

Ch. "PR" Byrd's Vicki of Parks, in a natural stack. On this day, she was judged Best Female TFT and Best of Show. Her proud owners are Ronald and Colleen Byrd, of Berger, Missouri.

128

trained. Traveling down the driveway is a world away from traveling to a dog show in a crate and then being taken to ringside where all manner of dogs are waiting their turn. Going back to the speech analogy, this is the spot where you might have had to visit the restroom. Yet we expect the puppy to put all behind him and go in there and not only perform well, but also win. This has happened, but it is not the norm.

We need to be sensitive to that puppy entering his first few shows. He will feel your pressure and he will note your disappointment. Please attend these shows with low expectations and be surprised if he shows well. Remember how you would feel under the same circumstances. Keep it fun for the puppy. Give him praises, hugs, and treats as he needs your support most at the beginning of his show career.

In your initial look at the litter, you should look for the extroverted puppy. It is so much easier to enhance natural showiness than to build it into a puppy. Of course, puppies change over the weeks. In a recent litter, the smallest puppy that had been picked on at week four became a cocky, game little puppy by week eight. Early on the larger puppies in the litter are the first out of the nest box because developmentally they are ahead of their littermates. Consider whether that feisty four-week-old might ultimately be larger than you would like. Look at the bone, especially the feet, as a key to this issue.

Hopefully, the breeder has been responsible enough to socialize your puppy. If this does not appear to be happening and if you live nearby, you might exert some influence by offering to visit and bring others with you to play with the puppies. Plan your strategy in advance as to how you will build confidence: Whom will he meet? Where will you take him? To how many different environments can he be exposed? I do know of a breeder of a larger breed who actually pays the neighbor's children to play with her puppies. Why couldn't I have gotten a job like that when I was young?

When puppies are old enough to follow you, it is time to put a very small, lightweight lead on them and encourage them to follow. There are various leads available and we have used several. We are currently using a toy size martindale lead. We like it for its ability to stay in place and still allow the handler to loosen or tighten very easily. After putting the lead on the puppy, he will likely go where he wants to go and its OK to follow him. Some puppies will feel the strangeness of the lead and plop down and refuse to move. NEVER pull your puppy on the lead. Pick him up and talk to him and then set him down in a different spot and see what happens. At some point he will move and you will reinforce this positively through praise and a treat. This is the pattern for success. Praise profusely and treat them, making this a fun thing to do. You may wish to gait a natural mover with the reticent pup to give the latter the idea. I recently was moving three puppies at a time and am still untangling leads. Keep your training time short at the outset—three minutes maximum—and

Jeri Singleton, of Annapolis, Maryland, poses her Gr. Ch. "PR" Singleton's Stormy Ace on the table. (Harkins photo)

work up to longer periods as he gets older. Puppies lose interest quickly and remember, you want to make it fun.

Eventually your puppy will be walking successfully at your side. The ideal pace is a brisk trot on a loose lead. TFTs are notorious for noting any hairballs or discarded bait that cross their paths. Above all, do not choke your puppy. Some exhibitors move their TFTs completely strung up, so that the front feet move in an exaggerated manner and the feet barely touch the ground. This hurts the puppy and embarrasses you, especially if the pup spits up and you end up stopping the show to clean the mat. Keeping your puppy's attention may be problematic, but a gentle correction by pulling up on the lead will remind him of the task at hand. Some exhibitors move their dog much too quickly, so much so the judge may ask them to move again, slower. Such speedy movement may animate the dog, but the movement may be disastrous as the dog struggles to avoid interference between his front and back legs. It may elevate the front legs too high, giving the appearance of a hackney gait, or it may side wind to avoid interference fore and aft.

I would advise you to gait your puppy on various surfaces. You may want to purchase a length of matting for practicing. Be sure to add several strips of duct tape to the practice mat, as many will jump over the tape in the ring if they have not experienced tape before show time. It is also important to practice on grass. Our first outdoor AKC show was a disaster because our dogs had been used to being shown on mats. Prior to this outdoor show, a walk on the grass meant potty time. Let's just say it was a difficult day. However, now they understand that when that show lead is on they are to gait as practiced whether on concrete, mats or grass.

The prevalent walk patterns for examining movement are the down and back and the triangle. In the latter, you would want a smooth transition as the puppy displays rear, side and then front action. Hopefully your puppy will avoid lunging for bits of treats left on the mat by previous exhibitors. When coming off the table, TFTs will often want to shake. If you start your movement too soon, they may stop mid step and shake. Some judges will have the puppy go down and back on the

Gr. Ch. "PR" Byrd's Mi-Treasure,
owned by Ronald and Colleen Byrd,
poses for the judge.

diagonal mat and then check side
movement. The problem for exhibitors
is moving in a straight line, especially if
they concentrate their attention on
their dog. The handler looks up all of a sudden to notice that they are not approaching the judge in a straight line. Use the judge the way a surveyor does the pole. Taking your eyes off your charge, check the pole (judge) and then move toward him checking mid trip whether you are still in line.

Move your puppy at a slow trot, stop when instructed to do so, and turn toward the puppy, breaking off a piece of a treat. Hold his attention for a moment and then reward him. This natural posing will be important as the judge walks down the line of dogs in the class to make a decision. TFTs must be taught to stack naturally on the floor, as handlers do not drop to the floor to stack as in some other breeds. Many judges will simulate breaking a treat as the dog is standing in front of them to see the dog's expression. As he poses, note whether the legs are under the dog and parallel to one another. You might need to move him a step forward to achieve a better stance. Gradually lengthen the amount of time before you give the treat. You will come to know how long you can hold such riveting attention before actually rewarding the dog.

It is obvious that bait plays a large role in the training of TFTs. They love to please their owner, but a little bribery in the form of a treat will insure their compliance with requests. In the ring, bait
helps to hold the dog's attention and
divert it from all the action that swirls
about a show ring. With bait, you
have an easier time capturing expression for the judge as well as holding
your TFT in a pose for him to be better evaluated.

Start stacking puppies early.

Judges in UKC shows have the option of whether to allow exhibitors to use bait, squeakers, or toys to maintain a dog's attention. Some judges see the use of bait as being artificial and prefer that the dog be shown naturally with emphasis being on the dog showing itself. Other judges would prefer to use their own squeaker to catch the TFTs attention, preferring that the dog look at the judge for an expression check. Additionally, it is a sad fact that some exhibitors throw and drop bait in the ring and never pick it up—a certain distraction to other dogs that follow.

The list of food items that work well is endless, but I have had the most luck with the following: cheese, liver, hot dogs, chicken, and commercial bacon flavored treats. However, there are four criteria that determine whether I take the bait to a show: The bait should not crumble easily; it should not soil clothing; it should be easy to handle; and it should not spoil easily. I have found also that what works one week may not work the next. In fact, some of my TFTs seem to always prefer what the handler in front of us is using! One TFT was waiting to enter the ring, but had his eye glued to another handler- the lure was teriyaki steak from last evening's restaurant. The next week it was chicken. I think it may do well to practice with one type of bait and additionally bring something special to the show to really get them excited. We practice with commercial treats with one bitch, but take fried chicken breast to the shows to maximize her performance.

Bait should be used in small bits. This is not mealtime. I recently examined a TFT with bait still in his mouth and on his teeth- not a pretty sight. It is better to cut your bait into small bits ahead of time and carry them in a small pouch on your belt than to try to bite off hunks in the ring. I often wonder how elegantly dressed handlers can endure having a cheek full of liver as they show. Of course, I never liked the taste of liver.

Some dogs will key on a squeaker toy like a furry mouse and can't wait to get it in their mouth for a shake. Such dogs get very excited when they see the toy. Heaven forbid they

This puppy is already comfortable on the table. Photo by Judy Threlfall.

actually get hold of the toy in the ring—you may not be able to take it away! Not all TFTs will react to a toy, but if yours does, this is so much easier than carrying bait.

Bait or no bait, Toy Fox Terriers are not generally comfortable on the table and for this reason I would start practicing this examination early in the training process. When I complained early on that my TFTs never seemed happy on the table, one of my mentors said "Let me put you up on the roof and send a stranger up to pat you down and see how happy you'd be!" It is difficult for a TFT to ever completely relax on the table. Short periods on the table without any attempt to stack them will suffice in the beginning. Using a two-person approach (one of us simulating a judge, one the exhibitor), we always go over the dog and look at the bite, praising and giving a tiny treat. Gradually the time on the table is lengthened and you can begin to stack the puppy.

Initially, just keeping all four legs on the table is an accomplishment. Successfully stacking the puppy and holding that pose takes time. I like to hold the puppy's head with one hand and put my other hand under the brisket (upper chest area) and lift the dog and gently drop the front feet in place. If the legs are still not placed correctly, you may adjust the position on the leg by grasping the elbow of each front leg, still holding the head with the other hand, then place the back legs by grasping the hock joint so that the line from this joint to the feet is perpendicular. I also note whether the back legs are spread too wide in comparison to the front legs. Most toy breed judges have a gentle hand and will pay special attention to beginning puppies. Some will wait to check the bite last if they think this will particularly upset the puppy. Hopefully by this time, you have been giving your puppy so many treats for showing the teeth, he will more than willing to let the judge or you examine the bite.

All of the practicing that you do at home may be for naught in the environment of a dog show. Call your local kennel club and inquire where and when conformation classes are offered. Here is the opportunity to train in a setting very much like the show ring. The larger dogs in the class may initially be a little threatening to your TFT, but as long as the large dogs are not allowed to run up on your dog, being around large dogs is an important part of preparing your puppy for the actual show. You may elect to not spend an entire hour the first time or two lest you wear out your puppy. In addition, if there are other nearby conformation classes you may wish to visit them also in order to expose your puppy to a variety of experiences.

As your can see, training a show dog takes a great deal of patience, ingenuity, and a degree of trial and error. Occasionally all exhibitors run into a puppy who just plain does not enjoy the show experience. The reward for your hard efforts, however, comes with those puppies that slowly catch on to what conformation is all about and display the wonderful zest for life that is the essence of the Toy Fox Terrier as they move with grace and style around the show ring.

THE VERSATILE TFT

In the past, the Toy Fox Terrier has been thought of primarily as a pet and a show dog. In recent years, however, more and more owners have discovered that their little dogs are amazingly versatile. As the breed grows in popularity, we will, no doubt, see Toy Fox Terriers put to even more imaginative uses. In fact, the TFT's abilities seem limitless. While it would be impossible to detail all the myriad services performed by TFTs, we would like to present a few examples. We salute the owners and trainers who daily break new ground for the breed. It is our hope that TFTs will reach ever greater levels of achievement.

TFTS IN SHOW BIZ

As we've mentioned, in the early 1900's, little Fox Terriers thrilled rural audiences in dog and pony shows. Today, Californian Marge Rutherford continues that tradition. Marge owns a unique troupe of toy entertainers. *Canine Capers*, as Marge has dubbed her ensemble, performs at rest homes, schools and homes for handicapped children.

It would be hard to imagine a person more eminently qualified to perform as canine ringmaster. Marge obtained her first purebred dog, an Irish Terrier, in 1938. This was an exciting time in the world of purebred dogs. The American Kennel Club had just launched the sport of dog obedience. Marge says that she learned to train largely by trial and error. Clearly, Marge learned her lessons well, for she joined the staff of the famous Hollywood Dog Training School. For seven years she worked under the renowned trainer Carl Spitz. Mr. Spitz learned his craft from German's illustrious Inspector Schultz, who was responsible for the widespread use of dogs by many European police units. So famous was the "College for Dogs", that the pets of many Hollywood celebrities were enrolled. It was while working for Mr. Spitz that Marge had her first introduction to canine entertainers. She handled the famous

134

PoHo the clown, alias Harry Corty, of New York City, and his talented TFT, Spartan, entertain the crowd. The TFT's intelligence and agility make him an ideal canine entertainer.

"PR" Hopkins' Loren Ace, one of Marge Rutherford's star performers, takes one of the steeplechase jumps. Photo by Tom Elder.

Saint Bernard, "Neil," in some of the episodes of the *Topper* television series.

After twenty years of involvement with dogs, Marge Rutherford decided to put together her own crew of four-legged entertainers. She opted for the toy breeds because they were easier to transport. The numerous props necessary for the performances were also smaller in scale. Marge is impressed with the intelligence and capacity of her little dogs. She says that what they can do is amazing. *Canine Capers* began with several Chihuahuas and a Pomeranian. The dogs play pianos, dance and walk tightropes. Several Toy Fox Terriers have since joined Marge's troupe. The photos clearly demonstrate Marge's success! The steeplechase has proven extremely popular. No doubt, Marge Rutherford and her performing TFTs have brightened the day for many people!

HANDI-TFTS

One of the most impressive and unusual uses of the Toy Fox Terrier is as a "Handi-Dog." Judy Guillot, of Tucson, Arizona, is a pioneer of this inventive use of the TFT. Judy, a medical technologist, is confined to a wheelchair. Through the use of her dogs, "PR" Meadowood's Jillian (bred by John Davidson) and her daughter, "PR" Casas Adobe's Amber, Judy's life has been made easier.

The brainchild of founder Alamo Reaves in 1974, "Handi-Dogs" was formed to train dogs to aid the handicapped. For the wheelchair bound individual, the Handi-Dog retrieves dropped articles and brings objects, such as shoes and newspapers. The dogs are also trained to bark, in the event a disabled person should fall. In addition, the organization also trains dogs to aid the hearing impaired.

Handi-Dog owners have discovered, however, that the dogs serve more than physical needs. Alamo Reaves speaks of the psychological advantages of a canine assistant. "When you experience a physical crisis, whether it be paralysis, loss of limbs, or crippling illness, you suffer psychologically, too. You tend to lose your sense of worthiness and to wallow in self pity. But a dog loves you even when you don't like yourself, and I find it hard to stay depressed very long with my dogs needing me and telling me in their own way how wonderful I am."

Handi-Dog owners train their owns dogs, under the supervision of a nurse and trained volunteers. Praise and patience are stressed. Dogs begin with basic obedience and graduate to more advanced training. Dogs who complete the entire course are tested for final certification. If they pass the examination, they become "Certified Handi-Dogs." As such, they are entitled to the same privileges accorded seeing eye dogs and may enter restaurants, work places, planes, etc.

Judy Guillot admits the trainers were somewhat skeptical when she entered "PR" Meadowood's Jillian (better known as Asa) and Amber in the training sessions. Other toy breeds had proven unsuitable. Asa and Amber, however, surprised the skeptics. Even before the training classes were completed, Asa's performance had earned a place for her and Judy on the Handi-Dog demonstration team. On graduation night, in a class of twenty-four dogs, Asa stood proudly in first place among the obedience entrants. The judge awarded Asa, the smallest dog in the

Asa and Judy during a competition in Tucson, Arizona. We should all be proud of this very talented duo. Photo by David Ring.

"PR" Meadowood's Jillian in position next to Judy Guillot's wheelchair. Photo by David Ring.

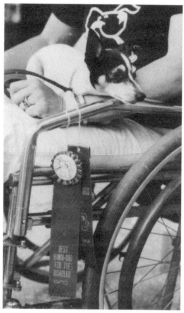

class, a near perfect score. She was proclaimed "Best Handi-Dog." Not to be left out, six month old Amber placed third. Encouraged by these early successes, Judy Guillot has continued to train Handi-TFTs.

"PR" Meadowood's Jillian takes a well deserved rest in Judy Guillot's lap. Photo by David Ring.

MENTALLY SOUND TFTS

CH. U-CD "PR" Fishinger's Elvis, owned by Nancy L. Fishinger, of Orlando, Florida, made history when he became the first male Toy Fox Terrier to earn an obedience title. Now Elvis and Nancy have done it again! Elvis is the first Toy Fox Terrier to have earned a "TT" from the American Temperament Test Society. He now adds the designation TT-1-TFT to his name.

The American Temperament Test Society was founded in 1977. This national-al organization serves breeders by offering tests which demonstrate a dog's inherent genetic temperament. ATTS holds temperament evaluations, in which dogs are exposed to a variety of stimuli. The dog's emotional reaction is evaluated by a panel of three licensed judges, and the dog either passes or fails. Mentally sound dogs must have the ability to distinguish between threatening and non-threatening situations. The tests are designed to weed out inherently shy or overly aggressive dogs.

The ATTS tests simulate situations that the dog might encounter in every day life. The dog and his owner are approached by neutral, friendly and threatening strangers, and the dog's reaction is observed. Reactions to strange noises and sights are also tested. The dog's willingness to walk on strange footing forms another part of the test.

Dogs who pass the ATTS test are issued a certification number. ATTS testing is one way to ensure that all TFTs will have stable temperaments.

THE HUNTING TFT

While the TFT is indeed a toy breed, he still retains many of the essential terrier characteristics. Lately, many owners are taking to the fields with their little dogs, to prove that they still possess these terrier attributes. Hunting with your Toy Fox Terrier is one of the best ways to assure that the breed's inherent capabilities will remain intact. Owners have also discovered that they can have a great deal of fun, hunting with their TFTs.

Some owners have shied away from hunting their little dogs, because they don't wish to endanger them. However, there are types of hunting in which even the smallest TFT can safely participate. Mousing is an ideal sport, in which almost all Toy Fox Terriers can take part. Since mouse hunting does not involve the use of firearms, it is a relatively safe form of field work. Mousing will afford an opportunity for your TFT to demonstrate the attributes of a hunter. For mousing, the dog will need good scenting ability, courage, agility, and endurance. These are, after all, the qualities that should be present in every Toy Fox Terrier.

If you have access to a field, you may want to try mousing with your dogs. Even puppies will find delight in this endeavor. If you're using someone else's land, be courteous. Ask for permission to hunt with your dogs. Once the property owner discovers that you are after mice, chances are he will be more than happy to oblige. In many parts of the country, mousing can be a year round sport. In the snowy northern parts of the county, summer is best.

Field mice are most commonly found in grassy overgrown fields. You may also want to check in fence rows, as

Ch. "PR" Cody's Eirwin Royal Billy climbs a tree, in search of a squirrel. His owners, W. D. and Dorothy Cody, of Tulsa, Oklahoma, tell us that Billy caught 25 squirrels this year. As Billy clearly demonstrates, a TFT can be an adept hunter and a show dog, too.

TFT fanciers Ernest and Gilbert Young introducing puppies to a racoon. Ernest Young has been one of this country's leading advocates of hunting with Toy Fox Terriers.

these are common places for the rodents to nest. It may take some practice to spot the mouse's nest, but you'll usually see a cluster of very fine grasses. Take a four or five foot long stick with you and poke the grass. Make sure your dogs are by your side. If you've found a nest, the inhabitants will scurry away when you probe. You'll have to watch your dogs closely or you may not be able to tell that they've gotten anything. Toy Fox Terriers can catch the mouse, kill it and leave it with amazing speed. If you find an empty nest, point it out to your dogs. Even though it's bare, it will still be heavily impregnated with scent. Your dog will often be able to take the scent and follow it until he finds the previous occupants. Encourage him if he does, for he's getting the idea of what hunting (albeit on a small scale) is all about. Most TFTs catch on to mousing quickly, but if your dog proves slower, don't give up. Just keep with it and soon you'll have your very own four-footed mouse catcher.

There are a few rules you should enforce to be sure that your TFT remains safe while hunting. You will most likely be going into the country to hunt. While mice will not be a safety risk, your TFT could be exposed to other animals. Make sure that he has a rabies shot for his own protection. Also, and most importantly, never allow your dog to hunt on his own. Most TFTs have a surprising amount of natural hunting instinct. Left to their own devices, they are likely to hunt in hazardous places. Your dog may squeeze under tree roots, scamper under a rocky ledge or go down into a small den. He could become trapped there and be unable to extricate himself. You, not knowing where to look, could lose your dog quite easily. Make sure that hunting is done only when you can accompany the dog. With these simple precautions you'll enjoy a day in the field with your TFT.

FLYBALL

Imagine a tiny black and white flash tearing down a 50-foot length of matting, jumping four hurdles in succession. The terrier steps on a spring-loaded box launching a tennis ball. He snatches the ball, which is as big as his head, and completes his

Foxlove Howdy Rowdy, the number one Flyball TFT in the U. S. Photo by Frank Jansen.

run by barreling back over the hurdles while carrying the tennis ball to the finish line. The spectators roar their approval as the smallest dog in competition completes his run flawlessly. Meet Foxlore Howdy Rowdy, the number one Flyball TFT in the United States, owned and trained by Sarah Stewart.

Flyball is a fast-paced canine activity in which four dogs sequentially run the course, hoping to be the first team to complete it without error. Flyball championship points are earned based upon the team's time, leading to prestigious flyball titles. Rowdy is the only TFT to have obtained his Flyball Master Champion title and is closing in on his next title, the ONYX award. Sarah Stewart notes, "Rowdy was a natural at flyball and after just a couple of months of training, he competed in his first tournament where he was flawless the entire weekend (this is not typical!)."

Rowdy may be a quick study at flyball, but Stewart believes virtually any dog can learn flyball, as long as he is healthy and non-aggressive. However, what Rowdy mastered in two months may take as much as two years with other dogs. Some dogs cannot avoid the temptation of leaving their lane to chase other dogs. Others do not want to return the ball. Yet these same dogs can become among the fastest when paired with a patient trainer.

The ideal TFT flyball candidate will be high energy. Rowdy's breeder, Chryste Gettman Psik, remembers, "I believed he'd be a great flyball dog because he was so ball driven, non-stop, and athletic. He was actually wearing a trench along my side fence! Rowdy really needed a job and he got one he adores." In fact, Rowdy often runs on two teams on the same day, scoring his fastest time on his final run.

A larger type TFT with excellent structure and in good, hard condition may do best at flyball. Longer legs allow speed down and back the lane and ease in jumping the hurdles eight times on the typical course. Such a sport dog may appear to be thinner than a pet TFT, but a flyball speedster cannot tolerate an ounce of fat or risk injury in competition.

The puppy that loves to carry toys and especially tennis balls in his mouth at an early age may grow to be a likely flyball prospect. Some TFTs love to quickly grab a tennis ball and run the yard with it while others never choose to do so. Similarly, the pup that enjoys a good game of tug of war may also do well. It is extremely difficult for many dogs (and especially terriers) to be motivated to complete the run once they have the tennis ball. Why should he gallop back to his owner now only to relinquish the ball? The tug and tussle pup knows that the best part is ahead, because the most fun in the world awaits him when he completes the run and the tug toy comes out for play. Of course, breeders can help develop these two characteristics by giving the puppies very small tennis balls to play with and encouraging vigorous tug of war games.

The ability to focus and attend to his handler's wishes is another important attribute. The pup that looks you in the face, his entire rear end shaking side to side, and who adores you totally may be best at maintaining focus. The distractions in training and competition are many—spectator noise, other handlers, and certainly other dogs. The focused TFT, filtering out the distractions, will be driven to return to his handler for praise and reward. Other dogs may find it more exciting to chase a dog in an adjacent lane. Such behavior can only be extinguished by making the chase boring. All action must stop as the owner of the chased dog holds his dog motionless. The only sound apparent is the chaser's owner who is making noises, playing with his favorite toys, and is now far more interesting than the dog that was being chased. Certainly this bad habit can be overcome over time. However, identifying the focused puppy and building a bond with him may alleviate the need for such time consuming training.

Training for flyball may begin in reverse. In other words, the last return from the flyball box is the first goal to be achieved. The dog has to want to complete the run quickly to receive his reward. The handler will ask a helper to hold his dog while he walks six feet down the mat. The handler calls the dog and rewards him with his favorite game of tug, a special toy or food treat. The dog must never forget his sense of purpose in finishing as soon as possible to receive his reward. With successful returns, distances are lengthened until the excited dog returns the entire length of the mat. The reward is given only after the handler grasps the dog's collar. The ability to control your excited dog after its run is essential.

Hurdles may then be introduced. The hurdles will be set four inches below the withers of the smallest canine on the team. The minimum height is eight inches. Thus, on average, the TFT will jump eight-inch hurdles. TFTs could become attractive height dogs for flyball teams since these dogs lower the hurdles for every dog on the team. This allows the other three medium and larger dogs on the team to accrue extremely fast times. Hurdling seems to come easily to TFTs. They are naturally adept at jumping and love to do so. Sitting on the other side of a hurdle with a reward will cause most TFTs to jump considerably higher than eight inches.

The first jump is placed six feet from the starting line while the rest are at ten-foot spacings. These spacings must be measured exactly, so that the jumps become a conditioned response and speed can be maintained. Again it is recommended that you train in reverse, with the dog first learning to jump what would be his finishing jump. Then add the second to last hurdle and so forth until all four are being successfully jumped in order. The key is to start with one hurdle and repeat twenty to thirty times before proceeding to the next hurdle.

The next step will be to start completing down and back trips over the hurdles. Place a tennis ball where the flyball box would be and encourage your dog to pick it up and run back to the finish line. When this goal is accomplished, the flyball box may be put in place. Throw a ball to the box loader and allow the dog to move forward, triggering the ball mechanism. Whether the dog catches the ball or not, the handler should lavish praise when the ball is actually in the dog's jaws. The command "hit it" is often used to encourage the dog to trigger the box.

This cursory introduction to flyball training could never replace the benefit of weekly training sessions with professional trainers. In such sessions each dog will be assessed and will work on aspects of their runs for improvement. While new dogs practice running hurdles, experienced dogs may be practicing efficient turning at the flyball box in order to improve their times.

The most expensive piece of flyball equipment is the flyball box, costing $300—$500. Most teams will have two in the event one breaks and these may be borrowed for at home practice. Jumps may be easily and inexpensively constructed for a back yard course. The smaller tennis ball is more adaptable for TFT use, but they will valiantly carry a larger one if necessary. Training sessions are offered at most obedience clubs. If not, these are the folks who will be able to refer you to a flyball-training club.

Attend a flyball contest and you'll be astonished at how much the dogs enjoy themselves. The bond that develops between the dog and handler is extremely close. They are truly a team. Sarah Stewart said it best, "Rowdy will always hold a special place in my heart because I didn't expect this from him. I took him to practice and while my team was very nice in helping me train him, not a single person expected him to be the terrific flyball dog he is today. He tears up and down those flyball lanes like his life depends on it. He goes to every tournament with me and I carry him in a front pack since he gets cold so fast and I look like a complete idiot doing so, but I don't care- he's my flyball dog. And I love him."

BOOGER: THERAPY TFT

In 1859 Florence Nightingale wrote, "a small pet animal is often an excellent companion for the sick, for long chronic cases especially." She recommended that patients care for their pets, because she believed that this was beneficial to recovery. The research that links dog ownership with physical and mental health has been firmly established since that time. We know that interacting with a dog can reduce the risk of heart disease, lower blood pressure, and cut cholesterol, regardless of the amount one exercises. Dog owners visit physicians less than non-dog owners and live longer than those without a canine companion.

If dog ownership can keep us happy and healthy, then one can imagine the effect of non-dog interaction for those in hospitals and nursing homes. Again, the research is clear- patient interaction with a dog decreases blood pressure, heart rate, and stress levels. Additionally, improvements in emotional well being and social interaction have been correlated positively with interaction with a therapy dog. Sometimes the benefits of a therapy dog visit may exceed what even medical science has accomplished. For example, there are accounts of patients who have not spoken for weeks and been totally non-responsive to any stimuli who immediately begin petting and talking to a visiting dog. After a canine visit, patients also routinely experience reductions in anger, hostility, tension, and anxiety.

Chip Fair's three-year old TFT, AKC CH UKC GRCH Foxchase Fair Bit'O Struten, TDI, CGC or Booger, was naturally suited for therapy visits. Chip says, "Booger has been a 'hands on' member of the family since birth. He has always been around people, taken to new and different places, and spent a lot of time in my lap. Booger has been training me in obedience classes for a year and he loves to work on his backyard agility course. These activities have helped him become more confident and more eager to please me, both traits of good therapy dogs."

The TFT can be an excellent candidate for animal assisted activities as a therapy dog. This is a breed that was so common in rural America years ago. Patients will naturally reminisce about their pets of yesteryear and many will recall a little black and white terrier that they had back

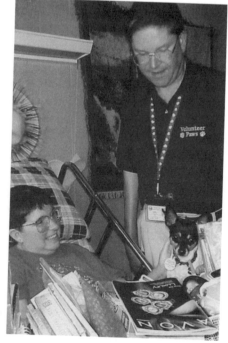

Chip Fair and Booger visit with Nancy Massey.

on the farm. The TFT is naturally compact and can easily adapt to the close quarters of hospital rooms containing medical equipment. Likewise, it is easy to lift a TFT to eye level for a bed-ridden patient. One doesn't have to worry that a TFT might jump on a patient and injure him or her. The TFT's short, easily groomed coat will please Housekeeping, with little or no dog hair left behind. Finally, the TFT's plucky personality, which persists even as they age, will warm the heart of the ill and the isolated.

It should be noted that not every TFT may be suited for certification as a therapy dog. Certification, from one of several national organizations, may be granted to those dogs that demonstrate obedience, appropriate temperament, and canine good citizenship. A quick search on the Internet will yield addresses for the web sites of these organizations. Of course, one can take a dog to visit hospitals and healthcare facilities without first achieving certification, but doing so could leave you personally liable if there were ever an incident involving your dog. Certification will allow you to either purchase liability coverage or be covered under your certifier's insurance.

The best candidate for therapy work will be well socialized and virtually unflappable. Hearing strange sounds from medical equipment and navigating around wheelchairs, canes, crutches, and walkers cannot be stressful for this TFT. The therapy dog should be well accustomed to being petted for extended periods of time by a lot of different people, whether staff, visitors, or patients. The TFT who loves everybody and craves the accompanying attention will be successful for therapy visits.

I cannot fathom a TFT under one year of age being mature enough for therapy visits. Jumping, licking, and streaking down hallways would be frowned upon! Some TFTs will mature earlier while others will enter a rebellious teen stage between one to three years of age. In any regard, the TFT should be beyond the hyperactive period and be able to attend to task. Stability is the key here. Retired show and obedience dogs would have the maturity and socialization to do an excellent job. A rescue dog that was neglected may crave attention to such an extent that therapy visits might benefit both the dog and the patients.

A basic obedience course is a prerequisite for therapy dog training. Your TFT must come when called, walk in an orderly fashion down the hall, sit, stay, and lay down on command. After successful completion of this foundation course, the handler should prepare his TFT to pass the American Kennel Club's Canine Good Citizen Test. This test documents behavior that all companion dogs should possess. Obedience training will be checked to be sure that the dog will obey the commands of come, sit, down and stay.

Stability of temperament is evaluated based upon whether the dog demonstrates that it will not shy away if approached by a stranger and will even allow the stranger to pet it, examine its feet, brush it, and hold the dog's leash while the handler leaves the room. The dog should demonstrate the ability to walk at ease at its handler's side and remain at ease while walking through a crowd of people. Finally, the dog's reactions to other dogs and startling noises are checked to see if aggressiveness, shyness, or panicky reactions are manifested.

Prior to beginning therapy visits, the health of the dog and the handler should be checked. An examination by a veterinarian should result in a health certificate, which documents vaccinations and parasite control. Dogs should be bathed, groomed (coat and nails), and teeth cleaned or brushed before each outing to a hospital or other healthcare facility. Handlers should have no active infections and all current immunizations, including a vaccine against hepatitis B virus and annual tuberculosis testing.

Each facility will likely have a coordinator for volunteer services who will interview the handler and his dog. The coordinator will check certification and health paperwork and may observe initial contact with patients. This coordinator will also identify those patients most likely to benefit from a visit and may schedule your visits with receptive patients. Other facilities have regular bimonthly visitations where dogs may visit several units. Chip Fair and Booger both wear hospital volunteer nametags while visiting. Chip also has a shirt that identifies him as a therapy dog handler and Booger has his own photo ID.

Caution needs to be observed with some patients. Patients with wounds or burns must have these covered during a visit. Tracheotomies must be covered by a cap or connected to a ventilator or oxygen source. Patients who are in any type of isolation or are immunosuppressed are unable to have visits. Parental consent is advised for pediatric visits.

Visits are often short, with the patient determining if there will be an interaction and the degree of interaction. They may just enjoy observing the dog and conversing about him or their own pets. Others will want you to hold the dog close for petting. Take care to avoid their contact with the dog's paws as some patients may have extremely tender skin. If the patient requests that the dog be placed on the bed, a barrier (such as a sheet or towel) should be placed between the dog and the bed linens. Many handlers keep one hand on their dog at all times. This ensures that the dog is always under control and enables the handler to intervene quickly if a patient gets too rough while petting or tries to pull an ear or tail. Needless to say, your TFT should always be leashed while working.

Your dog's visits may reinforce a part of a patient's treatment plan and goals such as improving strength, range of motion, balance, memory, and speech. A patient may brush the dog or throw a toy for him to retrieve to strengthen the upper body and improve movement and balance. Another patient might be encouraged to practice speech by naming canine body parts.

Jayne Healy visits nursing homes with her rescue TFT, Lucky. She advises that the needs of the TFT need to be monitored also. The TFT should be exercised before and after the visit with waste properly disposed. The handler may offer water and a treat before loading for departure, but never during a visit. Ms. Healy suggests that the TFT be watched for signs of stress during a visit. Panting, pulling toward the exit, or showing an unwillingness to visit the next patient may be signs that the dog is tired, bored, or having an off day. The handler might consider shortening the length of future visits to keep the activity fresh and fun for the TFT.

If you are interested in becoming a team with your TFT and visiting nursing and healthcare facilities, you may wish to learn more about the activity by contacting one of the national organizations or seeking out a local dog club that is currently doing therapy dog visits.

Jayne Healy wrote in *Fox Tales*, the newsletter of the American Toy Fox Terrier Club, "Sometimes I carry a Polaroid camera with me and take a patient's picture with Lucky. The picture is for them to keep close as a reminder that this little dog is a friend. Do not be surprised at the emotional response you will get from the visits too! Almost nothing makes you feel good about yourself like giving to others." Chip Fair concurs when he says, "Those of us who have TFTs love the breed. We enjoy sharing them with others. To be able to comfort one who is sick or in pain, to be able to brighten the day of one who is separated from friends and family, to give a link to memories of the dog they had so long ago—that makes therapy dog work beneficial to everyone concerned."

HOLY MOSES: THE SEIZURE ALERT TFT

By 1982, Daryleen Rascati was at the top of her career as a professional Arabian horse trainer. She had just garnered regional and national awards with her horses when she was sprayed by a crop duster while she trained her top stallion in a neighbor's field. She rode back to the barn to wash the horse and then to shower herself. Within three weeks the horse lost 300 pounds and almost died. Soon Daryleen was to suffer violent headaches, short-term memory loss, and then grand mal seizures.

Though the seizures became less frequent, the migraines so debilitated her that she could never regain her professional level of riding expertise. A friend and TFT owner, Dawn Benton, invited Daryleen to a dog show in 1991. She quickly realized that this was an activity that she could do and still indulge her love of animals as well as use her skill as a trainer. Daryleen chose Moses, a four-month-old TFT, to obedience train.

*Daryleen Rascati
and her life saving
TFT, U–CDX
"PR" Gorden's
Holy Moses.*

Darlene and Moses quickly bonded and he would sit patiently by as she endured the migraines; the seizures were now controlled by medication. A neurologist recommended a new medicine for the headaches with the unexpected side effect of neutralizing the seizure meds. She now suffered 15-20 seizures per day and she even fell on Moses several times. He would no longer sit near her but would jump on and off her lap for a quick hug.

It was 3 months before the seizures were controlled enough for Moses to begin his obedience training. During a class, Moses ran in front of her shaking his head as she felt a seizure begin. She was able to slowly lower herself to the floor, avoiding a fall and possible injury. Thereafter, Moses would come and signal just prior to the onset of a seizure.

Amazingly, Moses did not have to be in the same room with Daryleen to detect a seizure. Once he tore in from outside and jumped at her repeatedly, pushing her back into a carpeted hallway where she had time to lay down and await the seizure. Without Moses, she would have been stricken in a room with a hard slate surface. Since Moses did not have to be in the same room, he could not have picked up on a pre-seizure mannerism. Research had indicated that sensitivity to seizures might indicate a special ability to catch a nonverbal cue prior to seizure. However, Daryleen believes that it is more likely that the dog's sensitive nose detects an odor produced by a change in body chemistry. This odor has been noted by patients just prior to a seizure. The sensitivity that Moses developed to protect himself evolved into a measure to also protect his mistress. In 13 years Moses has never failed to warn of an impending seizure- once even breaking a sit in an obedience ring to do so. When conflicted between his keen ability in obedience and his devotion to his owner, there was no doubt which impulse he would obey. Though titled with a U-CDX in obedience, it is Moses' designation as a Certified Seizure Alert Dog that truly sets him apart.

AGILITY AND THE TOY FOX TERRIER

My introduction to agility came during a conformation training class. The agility equipment had been set up prior to class in the next ring and I thought that it looked like the circus had come to town. Midway through our session I heard a little dog's excited bark and turned to see a TFT starting his run. He was having so much fun and worked so eagerly. I looked down at my little guy and felt guilty, for he was not having nearly as much fun. I was just hoping that he would walk at a straight trot for the judge while the TFT in the next ring jumped hoops, rode the teeter-totter, and tore through a tunnel. The agility TFT was Shaun, handled by Barb Scanlan.

Although David Ring and Judy Guillot of Tucson have three of our former puppies trained in agility, I had seen them work only in pictures. After seeing Shaun, I was sure that this was an activity where the athleticism and intense nature of this breed would find an outlet.

As I watched Shaun's run, I was reminded of Olympic equestrian competition whereby a horse and rider go from one jumping station to another, racing the clock while minimizing deductions for knocking down rails and such. Indeed, my investigation revealed that it was an English gentleman with an equine background that originated the sport. Responding to a need for some doggy entertainment at Crufts in 1978, John Varley worked with dog trainers to devise a canine obstacle course. The rest is history, as this sport gained popularity worldwide.

In agility, the handler races against the clock to run the obstacle course in the fastest possible time. However, running the course clean or without error is just as important. In novice and open classes, a clean run can qualify despite a time fault. The course is arranged at random at each trial by the judge. Typical obstacles may be:

1. Tunnels arranged in various shapes; there is even one with a fabric sock attached, out of which the dog must wriggle;
2. Jumps over a bar, through a tire, or over flat slats on the ground;
3. Dog walks that test balance as the dog walks up a plank, across another and walks down still another;
4. Ramps fastened together to create a hill over which the canine must climb (A-Frames);
5. Weave poles placed about 20-24 inches apart with the dog threading his way through—a crowd-pleasing obstacle;
6. A raised platform upon which the dog must lie down for a 5-second respite.

It is important to note that height at the shoulder determines how high a TFT must jump, with 12 inches being average. Large breeds may jump cross bar jumps set at 30 inches.

A perfect jump for Lani. Owned and handled by John David Zieba. Photo by Sirius Photography.

Why is the TFT a grand candidate for agility ring? Barb Scanlon wrote, "The same characteristics that led it to being carried over the Cumberland Gap make it a breed with the gameness and athleticism to excel at sports like agility." Similarly, Kathy Stump wrote in *Fox Tales*, "Any TFT can do agility. TFTs are naturals at jumping and climbing at the speed of light." Even though most TFTs possess the raw talent to succeed in agility, the most competitive TFTs are unflappable, focused, and eager to please. The wildest puppy in the litter may be athletic, but sometimes those with most terrier personalities are a challenge to train. Can every TFT make a great competition agility contestant? No more so than every TFT who takes an obedience class achieves his competition titles. However, all TFTs can enjoy agility to some degree. Sally Richerson says, "Shy, timid dogs may not be the best candidates, but they do it and agility training will help tremendously to overcome their fears and build confidence and help them become much happier, healthier pets. It does wonders for shy, timid handlers too!" Frankly, more often than not in this sport, it will be the trainer's skill and dedication that takes the TFT to the competition level. If one chooses to not compete, he can still set up some safe, inexpensive obstacles in the backyard and enjoy the activity. Just as all children enjoy visiting a playground, all TFTs can delight in this activity to some degree.

What's in it for the TFT owner? Agility increases the bond between you and your dog as you begin to work as team. It can not be emphasized enough that this is a team sport, as Sally Richerson observed, "Handling skills for the human team member take a lot longer to learn than it takes the dog to learn obstacles. That's what keeps it interesting and challenging for people." It is also a way for both of you to get exercise, share time, and learn about each other. Kathy Stump advises, "Get out and play with your TFT. Agility is just as much fun for the handler as the dog!" Judy Guillot of Tucson, AZ says agility enhanced the bonding with her TFT, "I've never been as close to a dog as I have to Simone. She and I have learned how to trust each other. She has taught me

Shaun loved and trained by Barb Scanlan. Photo by Skipper Productions.

more than I've ever taught her. I never realized how many expressions she had. I learned to read her, her eyes, her posture, her ears, her stance, and her tail. She is amazing." Even if agility were not great fun, Ms. Guillot's rationale strikes to the heart of why we are involved with canines.

Agility training begins with obedience. Hopefully, you will have enrolled in puppy training classes as soon as your puppy was eligible. Likewise, a basic course in obedience for the adolescent TFT is a good idea. Of course, one can teach the basics at home, but it is important that your TFT be socialized to other people, dogs, and settings in preparation for agility. You may have to consult other toy breed owners for instructors that are good with smaller dogs and that emphasize positive rather than punitive techniques. The obedience experience should not be a negative experience lest the attitude transfer itself to agility classes. Confidence is a key ingredient to successful competition. Your TFT needs to accompany you everywhere and interact with as many people as you can introduce. Fortunately, this is a very portable breed that is welcome where larger breeds might not be allowed.

There are obvious reasons for obedience training. Some agility instructors will require obedience training as a prerequisite for entry in the agility class. Some may even evaluate whether your TFT is sufficiently trained to enter the class and lacks sufficient dog aggression. One club requires that the agility applicant remains calm and does not charge when a small dog is walked five feet away. Another exercise has dogs and owners face each other about ten feet apart. One at a time an owner goes to the end of the gauntlet and calls his dog who is being held at the other end. The dog must go directly to his owner to pass the exercise.

Eventually your TFT will be off lead in a larger group of dogs and you must be able to control him. Basic commands as stay, come, and sit take on very practical implications in such settings. Not all training areas may be fenced, so a good recall is an absolute necessity. As a part of the exercises, your TFT will be asked to wait on a table

Coming out of the tunnel: Lani Zieba owned by John and Connie Zieba. Photo by Sterling Photography.

for a few seconds. Here the importance of the down/stay (or sit or stand) commands are magnified. The ability to stay or wait is extremely important. Your TFT will have to stay at the starting line at the start of his run as you advance to the first obstacle. One can imagine the control that takes for an excited TFT who is ready to run. Perhaps the greatest benefit from obedience training is that the TFT learns to attend to his handler, to look for direction, and then focus on the task at hand.

Your obedience instructor can likely help you locate an agility class. An eight week class will determine whether this will be a fun, backyard activity or a competition event which will take you on the road to trials all over your state. In any case, one should devote at least 15 minutes per day to practice outside of class. You will likely build inexpensive jumps and weaves out of PVC and purchase a children's tunnel.

Lani does the weave poles handled by John David Zieba. Photo by Sara Nugent.

Lani waits for the signal to move on from John David Zieba. Photo by Ron Dawes.

Judy Guillot purchased a super fast chair to keep up with Simone—here pictured coming down a ramp. Photo by David Ring.

Competition agility may require two group classes per week and/or private instruction. The TFTs will become as hooked on this activity as their owners. Judy Guillot says, "All of our dogs thoroughly enjoy training and most times we have to stop them or they will keep offering obstacles to get us to engage. This is after they have been wet down and their tongues are hanging out."

Young puppies can be introduced to the tunnel early on and become familiar with the other equipment. However, obstacles that elevate the puppy off the floor could be dangerous should he fall. Limit jumps to elbow height or lower until those young bones and skeletal structure mature. Every dog matures at a different rate, but my best guess for TFTs would be in the 9-12 month range. Many agility instructors will not allow full height jumping or in-line weaves until the dog is over one year of age. A consult with your vet might be a good investment to determine your TFT's readiness for the rigors of training.

This early period of training with lower, safe heights is an ideal time to work on the basic commands you will use to navigate a course. You will be slowly developing a relationship with your TFT and a common language that will hold you in good stead when heights and speeds are increased. It may take six months to two years to be ready for competition at the novice level. You will note that the top performers are the result of years of training. Kathy Stump trained her TFT, Arthur, for 15 months prior to entering him in competition. In the November issue of *Front and Finish,* Mrs. Stump remembered, "The first 6 months he just ran amok. He was a true terrier! In the four years Arthur has been competing in agility, we have never walked away from any trial without earning a qualifying score of some sort, no matter what the venue." Arthur has earned 28 agility titles in 5 different venues over the past 4 years and was awarded the prestigious "MACH" title by AKC in 2004.

It is not my intent to teach each of the obstacles- that's why you go to class! As a teacher I have always believed that learning by doing (especially if it's fun) is the most effective instruction. I believe this is doubly so in the case of agility.

*Toy Fox Terriers are very athletic.
Jeannine owned by David Ring
and Judy Guillot.*

To be sure, you will be conditioning a canine athlete. Your TFT can not lounge on the sofa during the week and be at peak performance at weekend trials. Regular, vigorous exercise in which the TFT accelerates to cruising agility speed is imperative. Daily sessions of fetching a ball or Frisbee will allow the dog to stride out, turn quickly, and sprint going and coming. Above all, keep exercise periods fun so that attitude carries over to the agility ring.

Conditioning will also require the best nutrition available. Your agility dog requires the formation and maintenance of strong bone and muscle and the expenditure of extreme bursts of energy. Feeding the best canine food is the best investment one can make. I have often believed that dog owners in general supplement with vitamin and minerals too much, but I would defer to the veterinarian to examine your feeding regimen and to make recommendations for additions to the agility dog's diet. A pound may make a crucial difference in performance and freedom from strains and injuries. Just as cross-country runners are a leaner than average lot, your agility dog may be lean also with more tuck up and ribbing apparent. But the musculature in the front shoulder and rear thighs will signal that this is a performance TFT.

I would encourage all TFT owners to train in agility. The intelligence and athleticism that made the TFT so perfect for circus stunts can make the TFT a great agility breed. In addition the bonding that results from teaming with your TFT will intensify the close relationship between you and your TFT.

*Foxlair's Little Lucky charm bred by Violet
Denney and trained by E. E. Ward. Limit jumps
to elbow height in the beginning.*

THE TFT IN OBEDIENCE

 In recent years, the Toy Fox Terrier has made his presence felt in obedience circles. It's high time these little dogs were recognized for their intelligence and trainability. TFT owners are now realizing that obedience training is just as beneficial to a toy dog as it is to a larger breed. Recent outstanding performances by TFTs have done much to dispel the notion that this breed is too hyper and energetic to successfully compete in obedience trials. We all know that Toy Fox Terriers are smart. Obedience training gives them the opportunity to prove it.

Let's look at some of the day-to-day, practical applications of training. How many times have you opened your front door, only to have your TFT run out? If your dog knows the stay command, he'll remain in place when the door is opened. This command will also come in handy when you must open your car door. It's also very convenient to have your dog trained to come on command. Surely, you've watched someone attempt to chase and corner a TFT. The dog runs wildly about, darting here and there, just out of reach. With growing frustration and rising blood pressure, the owner chases the dog. By the time the dog is finally captured, the TFT is exhausted and the owner is fuming. How much nicer to tell the dog to come and have him respond immediately. This response might prevent him from ending up under the wheels of a car.

In addition to the practical advantages of owning a trained dog, there are other benefits. Obedience training is an ideal way to form a close bond with your dog. No other activity develops such an intimate rapport between owner and dog. You and your TFT will learn to function as a team. Most Toy Fox Terriers are eager to please and they genuinely enjoy learning. Training also helps to constructively channel this breed's abundant energy. Furthermore, trained dogs are generally happy dogs. They are a pleasure to take out in public and they help to give people a positive impression of the breed.

Jerri Lindsey and U-UD "PR" Adam's Beth, known as Abby, show the proper way to put on a choke collar. Photo by Warren Landry.

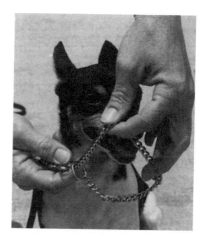

Jerri Lindsey and U-UD "PR" Adam's Beth, known as Abby, show the proper way to put on a choke collar. Photo by Warren Landry.

A BRIEF INTRODUCTION TO TRAINING

Obedience training your dog is not difficult. In many cities dog clubs hold weekly training classes, during which the owner is taught to train his dog. There are also numerous books, which give step-by-step instructions for training. By devoting a few minutes each day to working with your dog, you can have a well-trained companion in short order. Even if you have no desire to participate in obedience competition, your dog will benefit from learning the basic commands. While we cannot include in-depth training instructions here, we will give you an idea of how to teach your dog the basics.

For basic training, your dog will need a suitable collar. A slip (often called a choke collar) is best. For Toy Fox Terriers, a lightweight, small link chain, which slides easily, is preferred. It's also possible to purchase a nylon choke collar. It's important that the collar fit properly. When the collar is pulled tight against the dog's neck, there should be about three inches of spare collar. Contrary to its name, the choke collar is not meant to choke a dog. Used properly, it applies quick pressure to the dog's neck and is immediately released. Such collars are not cruel or harmful. You'll also need a leash. A five or six-foot leather or nylon web leash is best. Although chain leads are hard on the hands they do effectively telegraph any corrections to the dog.

Every dog should learn the five rudimentary exercises that are the basis for

Jerri Lindsey and Abby show how to teach the sit. Photo by Warren Landry.

all obedience training. The dog should be able to sit on command. He should walk at your side or heel, on and off the leash. He should be taught to drop, or down, when ordered. He should also learn to stay when so instructed. Finally, he should come when called. We'll describe for you, briefly, the basic methods of teaching each of these five essentials. Regrettably, space allows us to give only the briefest of instructions.

The Sit

To teach the sit, place your dog on a leash. With the dog at your left side, give him the command to sit. Hold the leash in your right hand. Pull straight up on the leash, while applying downward pressure to the dog's haunches with your left hand. Repeat the command so that the dog associates it with the action. Take your hand away. The dog should remain in a sitting position. Beginning dogs will likely stand up. Don't be annoyed. Place your dog back in a sitting position and tell him, once again, to sit. When he has remained in place for a few seconds, praise him. Be sure to tell your dog how wonderful he is for obeying you.

The Down

There are two ways to teach the down and both are effective. With your dog in a sitting position, give him the hand signal and the command, "down." You can give a small downward jerk with the leash and pull the dog down. Or, with one hand, pull your dog's front legs so they are extended out in front of him. With the other hand, press down of the dog's shoulders. As soon as your dog is down, tell him "down, good." Now, remove your hands from the dog. If he stays where he is, all is well. It's likely, however, that he will sit up again. Repeat the procedure. You may want to pet the dog while repeating "down, good." If the dog starts to rise while you're stroking him, tell him "no." Place your hand on his withers (highest point of the shoulders) and press down, repeating "down, good." This will keep him in place. When your dog stays for a few seconds, praise him.

Nancy Fishinger and Ch. U-CD "PR" Fishinger's Elvis demonstrate the down. Note the hand signal Nancy uses.

Nancy Fishinger gives Elvis the stay signal before leaving him.

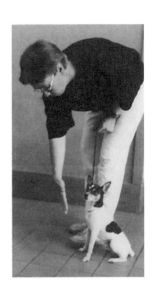

The Stay

This is one of the most important of the obedience commands and one that will come in handy in everyday life. Have your dog on the leash and place him in a sitting position. Stand in front of your dog. Hold the leash, partially folded, in your left hand. Hold the leash tautly, slightly behind your TFT's head. Give the dog the stay signal and the voice command. With the taut leash, you'll be able to keep your dog in place should he try to move. If he doesn't try to get up, take a couple of steps backward and let the leash go slack. The dog may get up and try to follow you. Tell him "no," put him back in position and tell him, again, to stay. Gradually, you will increase your distance from the dog until you are at the end of the leash. You will also want to lengthen the amount of time you spend away from your dog. The stay should be used with both the sit and down commands. Be sure to praise your dog when he stays successfully.

The Recall

Place your dog in the sit position. Tell him to stay. Walk to the end of the leash and call your dog. You'll note that in the other exercises, you have given the dog a single word command. However, since you want the dog to move in this exercise, you'll use his name first. In an excited voice, say, "Spot, come." Keep the tone of your voice light and enthusiastic. Praise the dog as he moves toward you. Most dogs will immediately come to you. Use both hands to reel in the leash, as he comes to you, so that he won't get tangled in it. Tell your dog to sit when he is in front of you. If your dog does not respond to the come

Jerri Lindsey and U-UD "PR" Adam's Beth demonstrate the recall. Photo by Warren Landry.

command, give a jerk and reel him to you with the leash. If your dog seems lack-adaisical about coming, give the leash a quick jerk and, with small steps, run backwards. This usually prompts the dog to run to you. As before, have the dog sit. Your dog has now learned to come on command and much praise is due him.

Heeling

There are a few basics to remember when teaching your dog to heel. The dog is always on the handler's left side. This is referred to as the heel position. In heeling, the dog should walk quietly at your left side. His shoulder should be in line with your leg. He should not forge out in front of you, nor should he lag behind. Your dog should be attentive and learn to keep up with any changes in your pace. If you speed up or slow down, the dog should, too. If you make a turn or a turn around, the dog should turn with you.

Place the dog in a sitting position, at your left side. Take a step forward with your left foot. Simultaneously, give a little jerk on the collar and command, "Spot, heel." Remember this is an active command, in which the dog will be moving. Therefore, use his first name first. Start by walking a straight line or a circle. If the dog starts to forge ahead or move off to one side, give a quick jerk and repeat the command, "Spot, heel." A small jerk, which brings the dog back in position, is all that is necessary. If needed, several successive jerks may be used, but you do not want to drag the dog. You may want to talk to your dog enthusiastically while he's heel-

ing. This will keep the dog's focus on you. Remember, you want the training to be fun, not drudgery. Now, halt. Tell your dog to sit. Be ready to reach down and help guide the dog into an automatic sit. Anytime you stop, your dog should routinely sit. Keep heeling with your dog, giving small jerks whenever he veers from heel position.

Next, you'll want to teach your dog to do an about turn. When executing an about turn, you want to either pivot or take small mincing steps. You should always reverse your direction by turning to the right. Your TFT may well continue on in the direction that he was going when you made your turn. As you begin your turn, give your dog a quick jerk and reiterate the command, "Spot, heel."

Nancy Fishinger and Ch. U-CD "PR" Fishinger's Elvis show the proper position for a dog, when heeling. Note that Elvis' shoulder is in line with Nancy's leg.

Your dog should also be taught to make right and left turns. Your turns should be abrupt and sharp in angle. Right turns are sometimes a problem. Simply, give the dog the heel command and a short jerk when beginning your turn. Left-hand turns are a little trickier. Since the Toy Fox Terrier is so small, you'll have to take care to avoid stepping on your dog when you turn. Early in the training, use the lead to let the dog know what is coming up. Take small mincing steps or brush your foot along the ground, when making the turn. If the dog starts to move away, a small jerk will bring him back to position.

Your dog has now learned the basics of heeling. Eventually, you'll want to try your dog off leash. Don't be too quick to try your dog off leash, however. Starting him too soon may set back your training. Make sure your dog is working perfectly on lead and paying close attention to you, before you try working off leash.

Unfortunately, the above discussion gives only the briefest possible explanation of the basics. We strongly encourage you to sign up your TFT for obedience classes. If none are available in your area, purchase a book on obedience and start at home. Both you and your Toy Fox Terrier will benefit from the experience. However, should you decide to compete in AKC or UKC obedience trials, plan on enrolling in obedience classes with an experienced trainer.

One final note regarding obedience training. Praise and correction are the basis for all training. Most TFTs are eager to please. You will build on this by giving your dog profuse praise whenever he does anything right. Always try to be consistent in everything you do. Variations in the way you give commands, or corrections, will confuse your dog and delay the training process. Keep the training light and make it fun. Your voice should radiate enthusiasm and delight. Never, under any circumstances, lose your temper. There will be times when you will become frustrated and angry. You'll be tempted to scream and yell. Don't! Hang up the leash and begin again when you've calmed down. Just don't give up. Patience and consistency are important in all types of training.

OBEDIENCE COMPETITION

The American Kennel Club and the United Kennel Club offer competitive obedience trials for Toy Fox Terriers. The UKC offers three obedience titles to dogs that demonstrate their proficiency in trials. These are the Companion Dog degree (U-CD), the Companion Dog Excellent title (U-CDX) and the Utility Dog degree (U-UD). A specified series of exercises is required for each competitive level. A perfect score is 200 points, and a dog must earn at least 170 points to qualify for a leg toward his degree. Furthermore, the dog must score at least half the points allotted to each exercise to earn a qualifying score. A Toy Fox Terrier must demonstrate his proficiency by earning three legs in order to qualify for his title. These scores must be awarded under at least two different licensed obedience judges. Jumping is required in each level of UKC obedience competition. Toy Fox Terriers are measured and required to jump the height of their withers. A complete set of the UKC obedience regulations may be downloaded from www.ukcdogs.com.

We would like to offer a pictorial presentation of the various exercises required in each level of obedience competition. We are fortunate in having two history making dogs to demonstrate these exercises for us. Our special thanks to Nancy Fishinger, owner-trainer of CH. U-CD "PR" Fishinger's Elvis. Elvis was the first male TFT to earn an obedience title, as well as the first conformation Champion obedience title holder. This little guy certainly demonstrates that beauty and brains do go together. Our deep gratitude also goes to UKC obedience judge, Jerri K. Lindsey. Jerri was the owner-trainer of the record breaking U-UD "PR" Adam's Beth. Abby was the first female obedience title holder and the first Toy Fox Terrier to have earned all three UKC degrees. Our congratulations to these pioneering owners and their dogs.

THE COMPANION DOG (U-CD) EXERCISES

Ch. U-CD "PR" Fishinger's Elvis on the "Honoring" exercise. The dog is placed in a "Down, Stay," while another dog performs the heeling exercises. (35 points)

Heeling exercises include the "Heel on Leash" and the "Figure 8." Here, Jerri and Abby perform the "Figure 8." (35 points) Photo by Warren Landry.

Elvis performs the "Long Sit." In this group exercise, all dogs are given the "Stay" command and must remain in place for one minute. (30 points)

Elvis shows the "Stand for Examination." The dog must stand still, while the judge examines him. This exercise is done off leash. (30 points)

Nancy and Elvis in the "Heel Off Leash" exercise. Basically the same as the "Heel On Leash," but there is no "Honoring" dog in the ring, and no "Figure 8" is included. (35 points)

Ch. U-CD "PR" Fishinger's Elvis is shown clearing the high jump in the "Recall Over the Jump" exercise. Here we demonstrate the dog's willingness to come to his handler when called, even when obstacles are present. (35 points)

THE COMPANION DOG EXCELLENT (U-CDX) EXERCISES

The "Honoring" exercise is included in the CDX, or "Open," exercises. The dog "Stays" while another competitor performs the "Heel Off Leash" and the "Figure 8." (30 points)

The "Heel Off Leash" follows the same pattern as that used in the CD competition. In Open, however, the dog is required to perform the "Figure 8" off leash. (40 points)

Abby, owned by Jerri Lindsey, demonstrates the "Broad Jump." (20 points) Photo by Warren Landry.

Ch. U-CD "PR" Fishinger's Elvis showing the dumbbell used in the "Retrieve on the Flat" exercise. The dumbbell is thrown and, on command, the dog must run out and retrieve it, bringing it to his handler. (20 points)

Jerri and Abby demonstrate the "Drop On Recall." In this exercise, the dog is left at one end of the ring in a "Stay." The handler then goes to the opposite side of the ring and calls his dog. On a signal from the judge, the handler gives a "Down" signal to his dog. The handler then calls his dog to him. (30 points) Photo by Warren Landry.

Abby shows the "Retrieve Over the High Jump." This exercise is similar to the "Retrieve on the Flat," but the dog must leap the high jump. (30 points) Photo by Warren Landry.

THE UTILITY DOG (U-UD) EXERCISES

The Utility exercises include the "Signal and Heeling" exercise. In this routine, the dog "Heels," Stands," "Stays," goes "Down" and "Comes," strictly through the use of hand signals. (40 points)

Jerri Lindsey's U-UD "PR" Adam's Beth demonstrates the "Scent Discrimination" exercise. The dog is asked to determine the article that has been impregated with his handler's scent. He must select this one and bring it to his handler. (30 points) Photo by Warren Landry.

Abby, with one of the gloves used in the "Directed 'Marked' Retrieve." In this exercise, three gloves are dropped about the ring. The dog is told which one to pick up and bring to his handler. (20 points) Photo by Warren Landry.

In the "Directed 'Signal' Retrieve," the dog is instructed to go out and is then commanded to stop, turn around and sit. He then retrieves one of three gloves and returns it to his handler. (30 points)

Utility competition includes the "Consecutive Recall." The dog does a "Drop on Recall" followed by a regular "Recall." (40 points)

One of the great crowd pleasers at obedience trials is the "Directed Jumping" exercise. The dog is instructed to "Go Out" away from his handler. He is then commanded to stop and sit. The handler calls the dog and instructs him to take a jump on the way back. Here we see Abby as she takes both the "Bar Jump" and the "High Jump." (40 points) Photo by Warren Landry.

APPENDIX I
TFT GENETIC DISORDERS

Ralph J. Rascati, Ph.D.

INTRODUCTION

A recent article in the December 2002 issue of the *AKC Gazette*, introducing the Toy Fox Terrier as the newest addition to the Toy Group, made mention of the fact that this hearty little breed suffers from few health problems but that a few potential problems are discussed on the breed's web site (www.atftc.com). Subsequently, an article in the January 2003 issue of the AKC Gazette, discussed genetic disorders in general, how the defective genes can be identified, and how genetic tests for those genetic disorders can be developed. It was accompanied by a table that listed the currently available genetic tests for dogs by disorder, breeds in which they can be tested, and which testing facility(ies) can perform the various tests.

I am going to discuss six disorders associated with the Toy Fox Terrier: Demodectic Mange, Legg-Calve Perthes, von Willebrand's Disease, Patellar Luxation, Progressive Retinal Atrophy, and Autoimmune Thyroiditis.

I defined a lot of technical terms in the articles in this series and I would encourage you to review them before reading the rest of this article. I need to define two more terms that will be important in the discussion. The first is variable expressivity. This term simply refers to the fact that different individuals with the genetic makeup to have a disorder may show variability in the severity of the disorder. The second term is incomplete penetrance. This terms means that some individuals with the genetic makeup to have a disorder will not have it at all.

Now that we have some common understanding of terms, we can discuss the specific disorders that occur in Toy Fox Terriers.

Demodectic Mange

Demodectic mange usually occurs in puppies and, in the common, localized form, is easily treatable, especially in short-haired breeds such as the TFT. The mite that causes the disease is found on virtually all dogs and is passed to puppies by direct contact with the mother. It is not an inherited disorder but a low-functioning immune system, leading to symptoms (demodicosis). In puppies, demodicosis is usually localized and easily treatable. The hair loss associated with it is usually temporary (unlike in some coated breeds where a more permanent loss of hair causes this to be a more serious problem). Some veterinarians recommend (some very insistently) eliminating individuals with a history of producing puppies with demodicosis from breeding programs. However, given the large numbers of affected individuals this could drastically reduce the gene pool. Furthermore, it is been our experience, and that of more TFT breeders, that once it has occurred in a puppy and has been successfully treated, it almost never recurs. Since it has no lasting effect on the health of the dog, it should be of little concern, beyond the ability to recognize and treat it, to most breeders. A more serious concern is the adult onset form of demodicosis, which is frequently associated with cancer or other internal diseases. However, unless the underlying condition is hereditary, there is no indication that this more serious form is itself a major genetic concern.

Legg-Calve Perthes

Legg-Calve Perthes (LCP; also known as Legg-Perthes) is a degenerative hip joint disorder with a result similar to, but a cause different from, hip dysplasia. It is extremely rare in the breed. It is believed to be the result of an autosomal recessive gene and thus requires the mating of two carriers to produce an affected animal. Even then, only 25% of the offspring of such matings should be affected. Because the gene also exhibits incomplete penetrance (i.e. not all individuals who have the genetic makeup {genotype} to be affected will actually be affected) the number of affected individuals is reduced even further. Since there is no genetic test for this disorder, little can be done to reduce the incidence of this disorder except for vigilant observation by breeders and elimination of affected individuals from breeding programs. Furthermore, the occurrence of an affected individual also identifies the parents as asymptomatic carriers. Breeders must then make a decision as to whether to eliminate the identified carriers from their breeding programs. However, at a minimum two individuals that have been identified as carriers should not be bred to one another.

Von Willebrand's Disease (vWD)

Von Willebrand's disease (vWD) is an inherited disorder which renders affected individuals more likely to bleed excessively because of the lack of a specific clotting factor (von Willebrand factor {vWF}) in the blood of affected individuals. The mode of inheritance has not been completely established. Some studies suggest that the disorder is an autosomal recessive disorder. However others have suggested that the disease, which has three forms, shows differential inheritance patterns for the different forms. These latter studies suggest that the most common form (Type I vWD) may actually be an autosomal dominant disorder with incomplete penetrance and/or variable expressivity. Therefore, animals getting the gene from either parent may show varying degrees of symptoms and will generally have reduced but measurable levels of vWF (1-60%). In the homozygous condition it is generally lethal with puppies dying before birth or shortly thereafter. The other two forms (Type II and Type III) are rare and are truly autosomal recessive disorders. In these two types, animals are only affected (with severe bleeding disorders) if they inherit the abnormal gene from both parents. Heterozygous individuals are clinically normal asymptomatic carriers even though they may have reduced levels of vWF. Because of the variable severity, vWD is often not diagnosed until the dog is several years old. There are tests that can be done. Genetic testing can be done in some breeds, but, to my knowledge, not yet in the Toy Fox Terrier. Testing for vWF levels in blood samples can be done for any breed. Severity of Type I vWD depends on vWF levels, breed, and age and therefore, are not always readily interpretable. The disease cannot be cured but, in most cases, can be managed. Management procedures include applying prolonged pressure to wounds, cautery, transfusions of vWF, and thyroid supplements if the condition is associated with hypothyroidism. Aspirin, ibuprofen, and other drugs that affect platelet function, and therefore affect blood clotting, should be avoided. Breeding recommendations range from elimination of carriers from breeding programs to only eliminating affected individuals.

To Test or Not To Test?

Of the three disorders discussed in this article only one (von Willebrand's Disease) can actually be tested for the existence of carriers. One (Legg-Calve Perthes) can only have carriers identified when affected dogs have been produced. The questions then are:

1. Where possible, should all breeding dogs be tested; If not why not?

2. Should all dogs identified as asymptomatic carriers (either by testing or by producing affected offspring) be automatically eliminated from breeding; If so, what will be the consequences to the breed?

My recommendation for Demodectic Mange is treat it but don't let it affect your breeding program.

My recommendation for LCP is that once carriers have been identified by producing affected offspring, do not use either the carrier parents or the affected dogs for breeding since this is a structural fault that we need to eliminate from the breed as much as possible.

My recommendation for vWD is basically the same as my previous recommendation for CHG:

1. Test your foundation breeding stock. If none are carriers then you never have to test any of their offspring because only carriers can produce more carriers (or produce vWD-affected pups).

2. If you bring a new dog into your kennel as a breeding dog, be sure that it has been certified not to be a carrier (either it has been tested and found not to be a carrier or its parents were tested and neither one was a carrier).

3. If you breed one of your dogs to one at another kennel, be sure that the other dog has been certified not to be a carrier.

4. Under these circumstances, testing is a one-time thing that you will not have to do again as long as you never breed to a carrier.

5. However, if you test one of your dogs and it is a carrier you have several options:

If it does not have other characteristics that you really want as part of your breeding program then don't breed it; have it spayed or neutered and place it as a pet.

If it has some desirable characteristics, but so do others of your dogs that are not carriers, then don't breed it; have it spayed or neutered and place it as a pet; use the other, non-carrier dogs instead.

If, in the rare circumstance that it has desirable characteristics that you do not have in other dogs, or that you know from previous breedings it readily passes on to its offspring, then breed it (but not to another carrier). However, remember that if you do breed it (even to a non-carrier), you should, as an ethical and responsible breeder, test any offspring that will be kept or sold as breeding stock, since they have the potential to also be carriers. You should also inform prospective buyers of the results. If you do not want to test such offspring yourself then you should at least inform prospective buyers that the offspring may be vWD carriers and let the buyers make an informed decision as to whether to buy. Remember that you do not need to test puppies that will be sold as pets and spayed or neutered. Even though there is the possibility that they may be carriers, they will have no vWD-related health problems and therefore, do not represent any increased risk of veterinary expenses to the new owners.

The bottom line is that testing and elimination of carriers from your breeding stock is best if you can do so without losing desirable characteristics that you may have worked long and hard to bring into your breeding lines. If you cannot eliminate a carrier without losing something else important to your breeding program, then at the very least don't breed that dog to another carrier and be prepared to test all offspring that will be kept (or sold) as breeding stock.

Patellar Luxation

Patellar luxation is fairly common in small dogs including the Toy Fox Terrier. The quadriceps tendon (above the patella), the patella, and the patellar tendon (below the patella) should all be aligned. The patella moves within the trochlear groove. Ideally, the groove should be deep enough so as to not allow medial or lateral dislocation during flexion and extension. However, when the connective tissue is too loose and/or the groove is too shallow, such dislocation (i.e. luxation) can occur. Mild forms can go unnoticed because the animal can extend the leg and restore normal positioning and function without manual manipulation. More severe forms require manual intervention to restore normal gait. Very severe forms can become permanent. The more severe forms can be readily observed by anyone looking carefully. Milder forms can be observed by manual manipulation. There have been no clear, definitive studies that indicate that this condition is inherited. However, health survey information and anecdotal reports from conscientious breeders suggest that at least a genetic predisposition, if not a direct inheritance, is likely. Ideally, every breeding dog (or potentially breeding dog) should be tested. Dogs can be tested at any age by any competent veterinarian, but are only added to the OFA database if the testing is done when the animal is 12 months old or older. When looking at the OFA form, it has check boxes to indicate if the animal is normal or luxated. If luxated, it can be assigned a grade (1, 2, 3 or 4) and it can be indicated if the luxation is unilateral or bilateral, intermittent or permanent, medial or lateral. Currently, there are no statistics available on the OFA website for TFTs but the database was last updated in December 2002 so an update may be forthcoming soon. Any dog with Grade 3 or 4 should definitely not be bred. Grade 2 animals should also probably not be bred. Since Grade 1 animals have few if any problems until well into old age, they may be useful in a breeding program but their offspring should be closely monitored. One caution, is that if a genetic predisposition exists, it is unclear that offspring inheriting the predisposition will be limited to luxation of the same grade as the parent(s). Therefore, it is unknown if a mating between animals where one or both parents are Grade 1 will produce offspring with luxation no worse than Grade 1 or whether such a mating can produce offspring with more severe forms of patellar luxation. Until that information is known it is impossible to make an informed recommendation for breeders concerning the breeding of animals with mild (Grade 1) luxation. Only careful testing and vertical pedigree analysis can answer these questions and, so far, at least to my knowledge, no one has yet undertaken such a study in TFTs. If anyone is aware of such a study, I would like to hear about it.

Progressive Retinal Atrophy (PRA)

Progressive Retinal Atrophy (PRA) is actually a group of related disorders that result from deterioration of the retina resulting in eventual blindness. In all breeds except the Siberian Husky (where it is believed to be an X-linked recessive disorder), it is apparently the result of an autosomal recessive gene and thus requires the mating of two carriers to produce an affected animal. Even then, only 25% of the offspring of such matings should be affected. The number of affected TFTs and of asymptomatic (clinically normal) carriers is unknown but is probably small. Dogs with early onset PRA should not be bred. Elimination of the disorder would require that the parents of any dog with PRA be removed from the breeding program and all other offspring of that cross be tested (preferably prior to breeding). Testing is by electroretinogram (ERG) which can detect PRA long before noticeable symptoms appear. ERG involves placing a contact lens on the eye and 2 electrodes on the head and then flashing a bright light into the eye, which results in a distinctive measurable electrical signal. The strength of the signal determines if the PRA exists (weakened signal) or not. However, even though testing can be done before symptoms appear, it is possible to miss the condition of the electrical abnormalities not yet measurable. A DNA test that can detect clinically normal carriers has been developed for some breeds but has not yet been tested in TFTs. Unless it can be shown that the incidence of PRA in TFTs is actually not small, I would not recommend routine (ERG) testing at this time. Careful record keeping to identify affected individuals and, by inference, asymptomatic carrier parents is sufficient for now.

Autoimmune Thyroiditis

Hypothyroidism is not uncommon in dogs including TFTs. About 80% of hypothyroidism is of the form "autoimmune thyroiditis" in which the body's immune system fails to recognize the thyroid as "self" and produces antibodies (TgAA) that attack thyroid tissue leading to progressive loss of function. Recognition of this condition is difficult because symptoms are fairly general and include such things as weight gain; neurological, ocular, gastrointestinal, or cardiovascular problems; anemia; impairment of bone development; sluggishness; hair loss; cold intolerance; loss of libido; and infertility. Furthermore, not all affected animals will show all of these signs. The most obvious sign may be hair loss but the most problematic for breeders is probably the loss of libido and the infertility problems. If you have a dog showing any of these signs, especially hair loss and/or fertility problems you should probably suspect hypothyroidism and have the animal tested. Testing currently involves running a complete thyroid panel including T3/T4/TSH and TgAA. The latter (TgAA) is specific for autoimmune thyroiditis. This test will only detect symptomatic individuals and will not detect presymptomatic individuals or asymptomatic carriers. The mode of inheritance appears to involve a single, autosomal recessive gene. No DNA test for affected individuals or carriers has been developed. Therefore, carriers can only be detected when affected offspring are produced from normal parents. The lack of a DNA test for carriers coupled with the late onset in some affected individuals makes elimination of the disorder difficult. Fortunately, treatment is fairly simple and inexpensive requiring daily doses of thyroid hormone. Successful treatment will eliminate the signs. If treatment is unsuccessful and infertility persists then the disorder has essentially become self-eliminating (or at least self-limiting).

SUMMARY

Of the last three disorders discussed, none can actually be tested for the existence of carriers in TFTs. Carriers can only be identified when two clinically normal dogs produce affected offspring. These three disorders also share the common feature of variable age of onset including some individuals who will show no noticeable signs until well past breeding age. This makes elimination difficult. Of the three, the one of most concern to breeders and their clients is, and probably should be patellar luxation. This disorder has an apparently moderately high incidence in TFTs and should be monitored vigilantly. The structural nature of the disorder, coupled with the potential severity of the abnormality, suggests that there probably needs to be an extensive study, including comprehensive vertical pedigree analysis, done to determine the frequency and severity of the problem. The OFA database can help with this but only if breeders take advantage of its existence and have their dogs tested. The situation is complicated by the fact that luxation can occur in genetically normal dogs as a result of trauma. This injury-related incidence of luxation is not heritable and animals in which luxation is the result of injury should be excluded from any pedigree analysis. Furthermore, they pose no problems as breeding dogs. Unfortunately, the tendency has been to consider all cases of patellar luxation as genetic. Conscientious breeders need to honestly evaluate the cause of any luxation in their breeding stock. Only such honesty can produce the trust necessary to accept the word of a breeder when they indicate that a particular case is trauma-related rather than genetic.

Progressive Retinal Atrophy appears to be relatively uncommon in TFTs and vigilant observation by conscientious breeders is probably all that is required at this time. Autoimmune Thyroiditis is not life-threatening and can, in most cases, be successfully treated. In cases involving infertility that cannot be successfully treated by thyroid hormone therapy, the disorder essentially becomes self-limiting.

APPENDIX II
TFT COAT COLOR

Ralph J. Rascati, Ph.D.

Coat color in Toy Fox Terriers is both simple and yet simultaneously complex. There are two (some would say three; others would even say there are four) basic varieties and then some variations of the theme. The two basic varieties are the white, black & tan (often referred to as tri-color) and the white & tan. The third variety is the white & black, in which there is no tan coloration. The fourth variety is frequently referred to as chocolate. It is, in fact, a white, chocolate & tan in which the black pigment found in the tri-colors has been modified to produce the chocolate coloration. In UKC this last variety is not accepted primarily because the modification was first introduced through outcrosses to Chihuahuas. Other characteristics introduced by those outcrosses were so undesirable that the practice was terminated and care was then taken to breed for type. To the breeders at that time, any chocolate coloration indicated that some of the genes introduced from the Chihuahua were still present and therefore those dogs should not be bred. They still appear occasionally and their occurrence may well increase since chocolates are accepted in the AKC standard even though they are still not accepted in the UKC standard.

Variations of the TFT coat color include the degree of body coloration, the location of body spots, and the appearance and degree of ticking in which the underlying skin is pigmented but the overlaying hairs are white. In both the UKC standard and the AKC standard bodies should be over 50% white and heads should be predominately pigmented (black, tan, or chocolate) as long as the predominant head color is the same as the color of the body spots, if any. The concept of predominance also causes some confusion because on some dogs with a lot of body color it may look as if it exceeds 50% when you look from the side or from above. However, if you look at the entire body, including the underside of the barrel they may well have more than 50% white. TFT breeders often have differing opinions as to what is preferred. Some prefer few, if any, body spots. Others either don't care or prefer more extensive body coloration as long as it does not exceed the 50% specified in the standard. Locations of body spots and of white coloration on the heads are more explicit in both standards. Ticking has also been a source of confusion for judges and others because both the UKC and AKC standards are somewhat vague. The UKC standard reads: "Ticking is permitted to some degree provided the white predominates and general good looks are maintained." The AKC standard reads: "Clear white is preferred, but a small amount of ticking is not to be penalized." Thus it is left to the judge's discretion as to what constitutes the maintenance of "general good looks" and what constitutes a "small amount."

Unfortunately, the genetics of TFT coat color is even more confusing. Mating outcomes have sometimes been referred to as a "genetic gamble" because, like games of chance, genetics involves the principles of probability and with a few exceptions no one can predict mating outcomes with any degree of certainty. However, some general statements can be made that are supported by genetic analysis.

The most obvious observation to TFT breeders who have been at this a long time, and indeed the most predictable outcome is that if you breed two tri-colored dogs the offspring will all be tri-color, with the exception of the rare appearance of a chocolate. Based on the genetics involved, one would also predict that two chocolates bred together should produce all chocolate offspring. However, when white & tans are introduced into the equation the possible outcomes become less predictable. Breeding a tricolor to a white & tan should, by genetic probability principles, either produce a 50:50 mixture of tri-colors and white & tans, or, alternatively, should produce only white & tans. However, we all are quite familiar with such breedings that have actually produced 3 or 4 tri-colors with 0, 1, or 2 white & tans. In other words, all combinations are possible. This is because we are dealing with small sample sizes when we speak of individual litters. Probability principles are based on the most likely outcomes when sufficiently large samples are used. It's like flipping a coin. If you flip it 10 times you should get 5 heads and 5 tails, but you could get 6 and 4, 7 and 3, 8 and 2, 9 and 1, or even 10 and 0 for either heads or tails. However, if you flip it 1,000 times you are more likely to come close to the predicted value of 500 heads and 500 tails. Some deviation is possible but you probably would not ever get 1000 head and 0 tails (unless the coin is weighted somehow). So it is when breeding tricolors to white & tans. If both color outcomes are possible then any combination of those outcomes is also possible.

What about the outcome of breeding two white & tan dogs? While it depends to a large extent on the genes in the two individuals it is safe to say that if the two white & tans each had one tricolored parent it would be possible to get both white & tan and tricolored offspring from the mating, although tricolors should occur less often than when a white & tan is mated to a tricolor. If one or both of the dogs had white & tans for both parents, the less likely you will produce any tricolored offspring. This is largely a theoretical discussion based on the relationships of the genes involved. In practice, rarely are two white & tan dogs bred to one another because most breeders believe that to do so tends to produce offspring in which the coloration is not as rich in intensity as that produced by mating a white and tan to a tricolor.

Finally, we have to consider the extent of body coloration. The degree of spotting, and therefore, the extent of body coloration is a complex situation that appears to rely on what geneticists refer to as quantitative genetics. This means that the extent of coloration is not determined by any one gene, or even a small number of genes. Instead it is determined by the number of genes for spotting pattern inherited from both parents. Let's call these coloration genes. Because of the random nature of gene distribution during the formation of eggs in the bitches and sperm in the male dogs it is possible for offspring to inherit anywhere from zero up to the number of coloration genes present in the parent's DNA. The more such genes inherited from either or both parents, the more body color will be present. To use some arbitrary numbers, let's suppose that one parent has 6 such genes and the other parent has 8. Let's further suppose that each parent has less than the 50% allowable body color. Furthermore, let's suppose that after mating these two dogs 3 puppies are born. Puppy A gets 1 coloration gene from one of the parents and 3 from the other parent for a total of 4. Puppy A therefore, will have less color than either parent. Puppy B gets 3 from one parent and 4 from the other for a total of 7. Puppy B will have more color than one parent but less than the other. Finally, Puppy C gets 5 from each parent for a total of 10. Puppy C will have more color than either parent. Depending on how many coloration genes it takes to exceed the allowable 50% it is possible for Puppy C to have too much color even though both parents are within the breed standard. Given the cumulative, quantitative nature of body coloration, and given the principles of probability it is safe to say that the chances of producing a puppy with too much color are highest if both parents have a lot of color, are lower if only one parent has a lot of color, and are least if neither parent has a lot of color. Given this situation the reaction of most people would be to say that if you want to minimize the risk of exceeding allowable 50% body coloration you should always breed dogs with minimal body coloration to one another. However, there are two potential problems with this approach. Suppose you take this to the extreme and breed two dogs with all white bodies (no body spots at all) to one another. You now increase the probability of producing puppies that have mis-marked heads with too much white or with white that touches the ears and/or the eyes. Such mis-markings are disqualifications in both the UKC and AKC breed standards. Another problem that has been observed by at least some breeders is that dogs with more body coloration also often have darker and richer color intensity. Therefore, in striving for minimal body coloration the breed could lose some of the richness of color in those body spots that are present and on the head. To prevent either of these problems from occurring, it may be desirable to, at least periodically, if not consistently, breed a dog with more body color (25—40%) to one with minimal color (0—20%). This should hopefully maintain the color intensity while resulting in only a small risk of producing offspring with too much color.

All of this suggests that while you can tip the scale in favor of the desired outcome you cannot guarantee that outcome with any degree of certainty. The basic premise of the "genetic gamble" is that you "breed the best to the best and hope for the best."